G000067527

THE PRAYER THAT GOD ANSWERS

---

*Experience the
Power and Fullness of
the Lord's Prayer*

MICHAEL YOUSSEF, PH.D.

The Prayer That God Answers © 2013 by Michael Youssef

All rights reserved. No portion of this book may be reproduced, stored in a retrieval system, o
transmitted in any form or by any means—electronic, mechanical, photocopy, recording, scann
or other—except for brief quotations in critical reviews or articles,
without the prior written permission of the publisher.

10 Digit ISBN: 0977695131
13 Digit ISBN: 978-0-9776951-3-3

Printed in the United States of America

Dedication

To Sarah Elizabeth,
Natasha Anne,
Joshua David,
and Jonathan Michael,
Who have been my prayer laboratory
for the past quarter of a century

Contents

1

Why Prayer Is Easy

In May 1990 my wife lay in the recovery room as we waited for the doctor's report. Elizabeth had undergone a range of tests from our regular doctor, who had referred us to one of America's leading surgical consultants. Now, following the removal of a small lump, we were about to hear the results of the biopsy.

The specialist did not soften the blow. "It's cancer," he told us.

The next two weeks taught me more about prayer than I had ever known, and the first thing I learned was this: *prayer is easy.*

Do you sometimes think praying is an onerous burden? I assure you, it's not.

When cancer invades your life, you discover just how simple prayer is. No longer do you drag yourself to your morning devotions. No longer do you secretly crave the distraction of a phone call. No longer do you fall asleep halfway through your prayer time.

Suddenly you *want* to pray. You want to pray so badly you can't stop yourself from praying.

And you want God to answer.

Being a pastor gave me no advantage in getting my prayers answered.

In fact, it added a second layer of difficulty, because I knew I was in the spotlight. Others look to me as an example. If the pastor cannot pray effectively, what hope is there for everyone else?

Very quickly, then, I got down to the task of "spiritual lobbying." I knew God was in charge. I knew He had the power to deliver instantaneous healing. My job was to persuade Him to use it, or so I thought.

I employed the usual methods. I made sure I spent lots of time on my knees, taking every opportunity to remind God of my situation. I got others to pray, on the principle that the louder the clamor we made, the sooner God would hear us. My case felt pretty watertight. After all, God could not ignore this satanic attack on my wife. Surely He could not stand by while my innocent children suffered. And wouldn't a healing be a tremendous testimony?

"If the cancer has disappeared when we go back to the doctor," I assured the Lord, "You will get all the glory and Your name will be uplifted."

It seemed inconceivable to me that God should turn down an offer like that. Within a few days, I was already working out how I would break the stupendous news to the congregation. I was ready for a miracle.

But things turned out very differently.

DELIVERANCE IN THE LIONS' DEN

Our follow-up visit to the hospital brought bad tidings. We watched the surgeon slide the X-ray films out of their covers. For a moment I still expected to see his jaw drop in disbelief, expected to hear him say the cancer was gone. But it didn't happen. Instead he frowned and said, "I'm afraid we need to operate as soon as possible."

Far from being able to thank God for a miraculous healing, Elizabeth now had to reconcile herself to the prospect of major surgery and a draining course of chemotherapy. This was not the outcome I had prayed for.

And worse was to come.

One week before Elizabeth was admitted for surgery, our eldest daughter fell seriously ill. Within twenty-four hours her body swelled up so much that we could barely see her eyes. We called in a pediatrician, who diagnosed an allergic reaction to sulfa drugs and decided to check her into the hospital for observation. Elizabeth went to be with her the first night. I stayed home with our other three children and called some friends in the congregation. Within hours the whole church had begun to cry to God on our behalf.

At four the next morning the phone startled me awake. It was Elizabeth.

"You've got to come right away," she said. "Her blood pressure has dropped so low that she's gone into shock. She's losing consciousness."

As I put the phone down, I realized three children were asleep upstairs. I was the only adult in the house. I couldn't just run out. After wasting a couple of minutes desperately trying to think who I could disturb in the middle of the night, I picked up the phone again and rang our dear family friend Polly Peacock. She was over in minutes.

The drive to the hospital that night is etched permanently in my memory. I prayed the kind of prayer you can only pray in the shadow of disaster—a prayer in which you forget all the normal courtesies and hammer on the doors of heaven as loudly as you can. I'm not proud of the way I addressed my heavenly Father on that occasion. I wrestled with Him as Jacob wrestled with the angel at the brook of Kidron. And yet I know that God understood the depths of despair from which that prayer came, for He understands me better than I understand myself.

I think it was during that short journey to the hospital that the prophet Daniel's experience crystallized in my mind: Daniel was not saved *from* the den of lions; he was saved *in* the den of lions.

For every moment of that long, dark night, Daniel had to trust that God would keep those lions' mouths closed. Until dawn came and Nebuchadnezzar's guards pulled Daniel out, he remained in imminent danger. He had no way of knowing the lions wouldn't suddenly get hungry and eat him alive.

And so it was for us.

By the time I arrived, the hospital staff had pushed the emergency button, and my daughter had been wheeled into the intensive care unit. We waited five or six hours (it felt like years) for a team of experts to assemble and diagnose our daughter's condition—not as an allergic reaction but as toxic shock syndrome. To our relief, she gradually pulled back from the brink of death.

Yet no sooner had I checked my daughter out of one hospital than I was checking my wife into another. The operation to remove Elizabeth's cancer gave way to six months of chemotherapy, with all its painful side effects.

Despite my early optimistic prayer, God did not deliver us from the lions' den. Like Daniel, we had to endure our night of darkness and danger.

Praying Is the Most Important Thing You'll Ever Do

What did this experience teach me about prayer?

You might say, of course, that I got what I wanted—in the end. The danger is now past; two people I dearly love are still alive and well; and consequently I can quit lobbying God and go back to what I was doing before.

But this is exactly the wrong conclusion. It's true that I'm thankful to God for healing my wife and daughter. In that sense I *did* get what I wanted, and my prayers *were* answered. But that is only part of the outcome.

What I learned was the vast difference between my agenda and God's. At the beginning all I wanted was for God to help me attain my own goal. By the end I had realized what a wealth of far greater goals is attainable if only I will take time to be alone with Him.

You see, prayer is not meant to be a means of getting what *we* want.

If we think of prayer as a kind of hotline to God, to be used in emergencies only, we have not yet grasped the Christian faith. The purpose of prayer is not to inform God. The purpose of prayer is not to persuade God, or manipulate Him, or cajole Him. Prayer is about *surrender* to God's purposes.

That is why Christian activities that are not rooted in prayer can bear no fruit. Praying is simply the most important thing Christians do.

Jesus spoke of His relationship with God in the most radical terms. The Gospels tell us that Jesus rose early in the morning—often before daybreak—to commune with His Father. For Jesus, prayer and communion with God were as essential as the air He breathed. His food, He said, was "to do the will of him who sent me and to finish his work" (John 4:34 NIV). Here lay the innermost secret of Jesus' power—the daily and disciplined bonding of His own will to the will of God.

That is why Satan takes prayer so seriously. When did Satan come to tempt Jesus? When Jesus was praying.

And Satan does the same to us. Many people think of daily devotions as a time when Satan will leave you alone. The opposite is true. Why? Because Satan knows that prayer is the key to your power. He knows that prayer is the secret of your strength and your victory over him. If he can cut your power supply at the source, he'll do it. For then he will succeed in weakening you spiritually.

So beware. There probably is no time in your day more open to enemy attack than your prayer time. Satan is always on the move. He is always plotting, scheming, planning, looking for opportunities to slip under your guard, in order to deceive and defeat you.

Doze off in front of the television, and I guarantee Satan will leave you alone. Get down on your knees, and like lightning he will be at your side!

DON'T LOSE YOUR NERVE!

Let me give you an example of how Satan can kick back at us during our prayer time—and how important it is to stick to our guns.

In a small town in Kentucky, there were two churches and one whiskey distillery. For years the churches had lobbied and protested in an effort to shut down the distillery. They complained bitterly that it gave the town a bad name and encouraged all kinds of evils through alcohol abuse. Nothing had worked. The whiskey distillery—owned, as it happened, by an avowed atheist—obstinately remained open.

Finally someone said, "Why don't we pray?"

And so the two congregations resorted to prayer. Like most evangelicals, they had not seen this as a first option, though of course much praying had already been done in support of their campaign. Now, however, both congregations dedicated themselves to come together every Saturday night and pray specifically for God to shut down the distillery.

Saturday after Saturday they prayed, "Oh God, shut down this distillery. Oh God, this is a bad witness for you." Until one night, while they were praying, lightning struck the distillery, and it burned to the ground.

You can imagine what happened the next morning. The preachers in both churches were pounding and expounding the power of prayer. For days, people in the town could talk of nothing else but this dramatic, prayer-induced, divine intervention.

Only later did a problem come to light. The insurance adjuster refused to pay the distillery owner. The lightning bolt, he said, was an act of God, and this was not covered in the owner's insurance policy. Whereupon the distillery owner promptly sued the two congregations, claiming they had conspired with God to destroy his business.

Now just how long do you think the Bible-believing Christians in that town went on preaching the power of answered prayer? Well, you could measure it with a stopwatch. By the next day they had hired a heavyweight lawyer who vehemently denied his clients had anything to do with the burning of the distillery.

The trial judge said, "This is the most perplexing case I have ever presided over. The plaintiff, who is an atheist, professes to believe in the power of prayer. And the defendants, who are church members, emphatically deny it."

Take note: when you start praying, Satan gets busy. He wants you to back down, so he kicks back. But this is not the time to lose your nerve!

How, then, do you get a handle on prayer?

THE PRAYER THAT GOD WILL ANSWER

Fortunately, God has not left us to muddle through on our own. In a teaching recorded by both Matthew and Luke, Jesus Himself gave us clear directions.

Luke set the scene. We can imagine Jesus up on the hillside with His Father. Down in the valley the disciples were tidying up the camp and watching from a distance. They were probably thinking, *What does He do all that time?* They were mystified and intrigued. So when Jesus came down for breakfast, they said to Him, "Lord, teach us to pray, just as John taught his disciples" (Luke 11:1 NIV).

The first thing Jesus advised them was not to make the same mistake as the Pharisees. You don't win brownie points, He said, by praying ostentatiously in a public place. You're better off seeking out a quiet corner and praying where no one can see you. Also, there's no virtue in using fifty words when ten will do the job. God knows what you need before you ask Him. What matters is to pray—not to frame your requests in pretty speech.

So far, so good. But then Jesus came out with one of the most familiar—and one of the most difficult and abused—statements in the Bible:

This is how you should pray:
"Our Father in heaven,
hallowed be your name,
your kingdom come,
your will be done
    on earth as it is in heaven.

Give us today our daily bread.
Forgive us our debts,
     as we also have forgiven our debtors.
And lead us not into temptation,
but deliver us from the evil one." (Matt. 6:9–13 NIV)

The New King James Version adds this phrase to verse 13:

For Yours is the kingdom and the power and the glory forever. Amen.

I believe these few short verses contain a gold mine of wisdom about prayer—more than enough to fill this book. But to learn these lessons, we must first avoid some elementary mistakes. And the first mistake we make is thinking we know the Lord's Prayer just because we have it memorized.

Some years ago, Harry Cohen was the head of Columbia Studios. His brother once came from New York to visit the movie mogul, and began criticizing the way Harry did things.

They got into a heated argument, and finally Harry said to his brother, "I bet you don't even know the Lord's Prayer."

"What does that have to do with anything?" his brother asked. Harry said, "I just bet you don't know it."

"Of course I do," replied his brother. "Now I lay me down to sleep, I pray the Lord my soul to keep. If I should die before I wake, I pray the Lord my soul to take."

To which Harry said, "Oh well, I apologize, then—I really didn't think you knew it."

The mistake is not as dumb as it sounds. What we commonly call the Lord's Prayer really isn't the *Lord's* prayer at all. Jesus never prayed using these words. If anything deserves the title "Lord's Prayer," it is the prayer uttered by Jesus at the Last Supper in John 17. A better name for Matthew 6:9–13 would be the Disciples' Prayer.

Also, although Harry Cohen's brother seemed able to rattle off his prayers like a machine gun, Jesus never meant for us to repeat these verses mechanically. Still less should we treat them as a magic charm. The words themselves have no power. And in saying "This is how you should pray," Jesus certainly did not mean for us to recite the Lord's Prayer as we would recite a Shakespearean sonnet.

This is clear from the context. First, Jesus had just taken the Pharisees to task for using meaningless and repetitious prayers, so He would hardly have told His disciples to follow the same practice. And second, nowhere in the New Testament do we find an instance of the Lord's Prayer being reproduced verbatim by the apostles. Had Jesus told them to, His closest followers would surely have taken heed. But no. The early church had no place for this kind of superstitious ritual—nor should we.

Now, if the Lord's Prayer was never intended to be a rote prayer, then what is its purpose?

GOD'S CURRICULUM FOR PRAYER

The Lord's Prayer lays out the curriculum for biblical teaching on prayer. It lists the study course and pulls together the major themes. It tells us what we will have to learn if we wish to master the art of praying. In drafting this curriculum, Jesus set out to keep things simple. We are not expected to have a previous degree or to have done a stack of background reading. Nor do we have to worry about being clever enough to learn, for the Holy Spirit, the third person of the Trinity, will always be on hand for personal instruction. As Paul told us in Romans 8:26 NASB, "We do not know how to pray as we should, but the Spirit Himself intercedes for us with groanings too deep for words."

As to the content of this course for prayer, at this point I will say only one thing, and it may surprise you.

Most modern teaching deals with the "how" of prayer. We want to know how to pray, just as we want to know how to access the

Internet or use a cellular phone. Internalizing that information, we think, is the secret of lobbying God successfully and getting our prayers answered.

But Jesus' perspective was radically different. In the Lord's Prayer, He focused not on *how* we pray, but on *what* we pray. Jesus' curriculum gave little room to technique. So, first we must learn to pray for the *right thing*—because that is God's central purpose in having us pray.

If you look at the Old Testament, it is evident that in crisis situations God's saints usually knew what to pray for. Abraham, for example, charged his servant with the duty of finding a wife for his son Isaac. This was no small task. Not given a list of candidates, the servant took ten camels laden with gifts and simply turned up unannounced in the land of his master's birth. Arriving at the well in Nahor, however, the servant prayed boldly. "May it be that when I say to a girl, 'Please let down your jar that I may have a drink,' and she says, 'Drink, and I'll water your camels too'—let her be the one you have chosen for . . . Isaac" (Gen. 24:14 NIV). God answered the prayer by bringing Rebekah to the well.

Centuries later the childless Hannah poured out her heart to God at the temple in Shiloh. Like Abraham's servant, she prayed boldly. "O LORD Almighty, if you will only look upon your servant's misery and remember me, and not forget your servant but give her a son, then I will give him to the LORD for all the days of his life" (1 Sam. 1:11 NIV). Again, God answered the prayer, by causing Hannah to give birth to the prophet Samuel.

Throughout biblical history, God's people have known not just *how* to pray, but *what* to pray. They were inspired to see the outcomes that would give God the greatest glory—because the "purpose of all purposes" in prayer is for God to be glorified. The act of praying may bless us out of our socks, but that is not why God asks us to pray. Prayer is God's opportunity to reveal His goodness and power, and to be glorified and magnified. Why else did Jesus say to the disciples, "And whatever you ask in My name, that I will do, *that the Father may be glorified"* (John 14:13 NKJV)?

Unless we understand *what* to pray to achieve the glory of God, our prayers will be ineffectual. The prayer that God will answer is one that we pray in a deepening awareness of God's agenda, not our own. It is one that we pray not from the urgency of our need (urgent as that may be!), but in surrender to His will and purpose.

I understand now that my first, desperate prayers for Elizabeth were not fully aligned with the will of God. They came from the heart; they were born of love. But I made a convenient and simplistic assumption that the most dramatic miracle would automatically win God the greatest glory. God knew better.

The Basics of Prayer

Before we begin God's course of prayer, we must, at the very least, take prayer seriously. And to that end, let me give you a few simple directions on the "how" of praying.

1. Give prayer adequate time. Can you imagine two people in love with each other, who talk only if they need something? Isn't that absurd? No relationship will grow if you get on the phone, give the person a list of requests, then hang up. If a husband and wife speak to each other only five minutes every day, the marriage will go downhill fast. And yet five minutes is—on average—how long most evangelical Christians spend in daily prayer. Five minutes! Be warned, however: you reap exactly what you sow.

2. Give prayer adequate space. Jesus did not tell us where to pray, only that we are to pray consistently and give prayer our full attention. Not many of us today will climb a mountain in order to spend time with God. But we can seek solitude of a lesser kind. To pray properly, we need to go into a place where we can concentrate without being disturbed. You may be the kind of person who can pray at the ironing board, with the television and stereo going, and with a telephone

jammed against one ear—but I doubt it. When Jesus advised us to go into an "inner room," He meant for us to find a place where we can focus on God and not be distracted.

3. Give prayer adequate attention. You can pray standing up or sitting down or lying in the bath. But to pray effectively, you will have to prioritize your prayer time. I know that is not welcome news to people with demanding jobs and small children, but there is no way around it. Prayer should be marked on your calendar.

Personally, I follow Jesus' example of rising early in the morning for prayer. There is no scriptural command to do that. It's just best for me because it lets me offer the firstfruits of the day to God. And I have to be honest: if I don't give that early part of my day to God, my whole day is miserable. I accomplish nothing. Of course, early morning prayer does not allow us to switch off afterward. We should pray in every situation—before meals, before meetings, playing softball, getting into the car—because prayer is both a discipline and a lifestyle.

MAKING THE COMMITMENT

Finally, let's not beat around the bush. When it comes to prayer, most of us oversell and underperform. We like the *idea* of prayer. We're just not so good at putting it into practice.

Most evangelical Christians today pray about like sailors use their pumps—only when their ship is leaking. When that happens, they work at prayer furiously. The rest of the time they don't want to know about the discipline of prayer.

That is the defining characteristic of need-driven prayer. The ten lepers in the Gospels exemplify it perfectly. In their sickness they all clamored desperately for healing. But when Jesus healed them, how many turned back to say thanks? Just one—and he was a Gentile.

When everything is going well, we tend to put prayer on the back burner. It is not our priority. We limit our commitment. We turn up at prayer meetings and say, in effect, "Oh God, please use me. Oh God, use me . . . but only in an advisory capacity."

We love to pray—if it's convenient. We love to pray—if it doesn't interfere with our busy lifestyle. We love to pray—if it doesn't get in the way of our Christian ministry. For, make no mistake, one of the principle blights on evangelical Christianity is our activism. We prefer doing to being; we value action over prayer. Yet prayer is what makes our actions—our ministry—effective for God's purposes.

God is not impressed by our activism as much as He's impressed by our spending time with Him. God does not desire our success or achievements as much as He desires our dependence on Him in prayer.

After all, God is the one who gives us the breath to go out and achieve and succeed. Without Him, we're dead. If we are not connected to God in prayer, all our feverish activity for the kingdom will ultimately come to nothing. Activism is dead without the power of prayer.

When you and I are in close fellowship with God, when we are intimate with God and at peace with Him, walking daily in the Spirit, then we will know how to pray and what to pray. When we understand what Jesus is saying to us through the Lord's Prayer, we will experience power in prayer as we have never experienced it before.

But it requires making a commitment.

I doubt there is a single person reading this book who doesn't feel a little guilty about prayer, who doesn't think, *Well, I know my prayer life could really improve.* If that resonates with you, then I beg you not to read this as just another edifying Christian book. If you do that, I guarantee that next month you won't recall a single thing God has said to you through these words.

Instead, make a commitment. Begin God's course of prayer. Resolve to look deeply into Jesus' teaching so that you can pray effectively. Because if Christians fail to learn both the "how" and the "what" of prayer, they will be in for a rough time.

I know, because I've been there.* I've prayed the wrong way, and God has started to put me right.

So please make an absolute decision that you will change your lifestyle and your habits. Whatever it takes for you to get up and spend time with God, do it. The Holy Spirit will help you, but only you can make that initial decision to change.

YOUR PRAYER WORKBOOK

Once I made that commitment to change, God began showing me how to use the Lord's Prayer—not as a rote formula, but as my pattern. The purpose of this book is to share those lessons with you. Each of the following chapters will examine one phrase of the Lord's Prayer in depth.

To help you incorporate what you learn into your regular prayer time, I have included a Prayer Workbook section at the end of each chapter. In the blank space provided, record your reflections on how each passage of the Lord's Prayer applies to your life; my reflections are given as an example. Then, after you meditate on the Scripture passages included in the workbook, use the space provided to record a prayer in your own words, following the model I've given.

If you make the commitment to pray, and if you follow the pattern you will learn from the Lord's Prayer, then God will do great and mighty things in your life. You will begin to see your most urgent needs met. And you will not just pray—you will pray the prayer that God will answer.

Are you ready? Good. Let's start at the beginning: "Our Father."

---

*While it is not primarily about prayer, my book *If God Is in Control, Why Is My Life Such a Mess?* recounts some of my early experiences and how God worked miracles in my life when I began to pray.

"Our Father"

2

Start Where You Should

Growing up in Egypt as I did was not easy. As the second youngest of eight children, I often felt lost in the shuffle. Twelve years separated me from my older brothers. Worse still, they were all spectacularly successful.

When I was ten years old, my father announced proudly, "Your brother Nathan has become one of the youngest deputy managers in the history of Barclays," the prominent international bank. Nathan was twenty-seven. From the way my father said it, I had no doubt that he intended for me to follow this example of success.

My mind reeled at the dizzying heights I was expected to climb. Yet my father gave me little help. In fact, far from having the freedom to realize my ambitions, I seemed to be everyone's personal servant. Throughout my teenage years, I resented always having to be the errand boy and always having chores to do.

"You must take my shoes to the cobbler tomorrow," my father would say, "and also help your sisters tidy the house."

"But . . . "

His frown silenced me. My father did not believe in doing things for his children. He had a rule: I did things for him, I did things for my siblings, and only then did I get down to my own business.

In stark contrast, my best friend's father did everything imaginable for him. Not once did I see my friend take his dad's shoes to the cobbler. His father ran all the errands so his children could devote all their energies to studying. During exams he actually met his son at the school gate—something my father would never have dreamed of doing.

So I grew up with two very different models of fatherhood. One was rigid and demanding, the other caring and supportive. And, of course, as my teenage years approached, I began to feel I had gotten a poor deal. *What would it be like,* I wondered, *to have a dad who did everything for you, instead of getting you to do everything for him?*

These conflicting views of what a father should be led me to a faulty view of God as my Father. For this reason I always struggled with the first phrase of the Lord's Prayer: "Our Father."

Your Heavenly Father Is Not Like Your Earthly Father

It seems like such a simple beginning, addressing God as our Father. After all, the father-child relationship is one that every human being can understand. Yet I found it utterly confusing. What sort of a Father was God? Was He like my own father, or like my friend's father?

It took me many years to discover that the answer to this question is "neither."

God is a greater Father than any earthly father could ever be. Earthly fathers just do not measure up. Even people whose fathers were fair, honest, gentle, generous, and strong will find their fathers' love only a pale reflection of the fatherhood of God. No matter how wonderful your earthly father is, he cannot compare with the Father of all.

Let's take a moment to see how far God's fatherhood outpaces the kind we get on earth.

Research proves that children whose fathers verbalize their love end up showing a high degree of spiritual maturity. So telling our children we love them makes a tremendous difference in their lives.

How much does God verbalize His love to us? We can be sure of this: our heavenly Father speaks His love toward us every single moment of every day. He is constantly saying "I love you" through the pages of Scripture, through blessings, and through other people. Through all these things He is saying, "I will always love you." He is saying, "Nothing will stop Me from loving you."

Another important aspect of the father-child relationship is what we sometimes call "contact time." It has been reported that fathers in America spend an average of only thirty-eight seconds a day being totally attentive to their children's needs. Thirty-eight seconds! And a further twenty minutes a day being *partially* attentive.

When I read this I wanted to shout—in fact I did shout, since I was alone at the time—"But my heavenly Father is attentive to my needs 100 percent of the time!"

The following statements are true twenty-four hours a day:

- I am the center of His attention.
- I am the subject of His concern.
- I am the recipient of His time.
- I am the focus of His planning.
- I am the object of His love.
- I am His total occupation.

Our heavenly Father gives every one of us His whole and undivided attention. When you pray to your Father in heaven, He does not say, "Not now—I'm busy." He does not say, "I'll help you in half an hour, when I've finished reading the paper." He does not say, "Go find your mom—she'll sort everything out." Every second of every day, our Father God is eager to help us.

And here is an amazing thing. This membership in God's family, this right to enter into the presence of our heavenly Father, is given to us as a gift.

GOD'S CHILDREN—AND GOD'S SON

A Roman emperor was returning through the streets of Rome after some great victory abroad. Tall legionnaires lined the route to keep back the cheering crowds. Finally the procession passed the platform where the emperor's own family was sitting. Watching the scene, his youngest son got so excited that he jumped down, burrowed through the wall of soldiers, and ran forward.

Immediately one of the guards scooped him up, saying, "You can't do that! Do you know who is in that chariot? That is the emperor."

The youngster quickly replied, "He may be your emperor—but he is *my father.*"

Not a mighty emperor but the Almighty God, the Creator of the universe—that's who our Father is. What a privilege it is to belong to God's family!

It is hard at this distance to put ourselves in the shoes of Jesus' contemporaries and to register their amazement at the easy way He called God "Father." The Gospels record Jesus using the term *Father* (Greek: *pater*) no less than seventy times.

Even more astounding, in the Garden of Gethsemane, Jesus addressed God with the Aramaic word *abba*. This carries connotations of deep affection, and literally means "daddy." With Judas and the mob approaching, Jesus prayed, "Daddy . . . everything is possible for you. Take this cup from me. Yet not what I will, but what you will" (Mark 14:36 NIV).

If we can call God "Father," and even "Daddy," it is only because Jesus has spiritually taken us into Himself. He alone is the faithful, obedient, perfect, sinless Son of God. He alone can truly call God "Father." Yet listen to the words Paul wrote to the Galatians: "You are all sons of God *through faith in Jesus Christ* . . . Because you are sons, God sent the Spirit of his Son into our hearts, the Spirit who calls out, "*Abba, Father*" (Gal. 3:26, 4:6 NIV).

Do you understand what an amazing thing Paul is saying? By faith we are made sons and daughters of God. No amount of righteousness or so-called good breeding can achieve that. But faith in Jesus Christ brings us a privilege infinitely greater than an invitation to meet the Queen of England—the privilege of calling God "Our Father."

That is why a Muslim cannot pray the Lord's Prayer: he cannot address God as Father. The Allah of Islam is impersonal and distant, completely separate from his creation, including man. "Allah has no sons" is a tenet of the Muslim faith. Therefore, Islam cannot comprehend the idea of ordinary people sitting around a heavenly table as members of God's family, for Islam cannot understand how God's Son has brought sinners to faith through the cross.

But let's be clear what faith entails.

You Must Name the Name of Jesus

Back in January 1998, when the scandals surrounding President Clinton first began to break, I stood in my pulpit and prayed that God would lead the president to true repentance and cleansing.

Later in the year I thought it might just happen. But when the president made his famous repentance speech at the September 9 prayer breakfast, I listened in vain to hear the name of Jesus. Not once did the word fall from the president's lips. Much was made of repentance; of faith in Christ he said nothing at all.

Judging from some of the comments Christians made afterward, you would think the president had fallen on his knees at a Billy Graham crusade. Yet saying you're sorry is not enough, no matter how many people see you do it. There is no adoption into God's family, no forgiveness of past sin, without the shed blood of Jesus Christ. Repentance on its own is only the first stage, just as admitting you're hungry is the first prerequisite to eating a good meal.

Without the shed blood of Jesus, there can be no true restoration. Without faith in the shed blood of Jesus, we can neither call God "Our Father" nor receive His forgiveness. That is the way He spelled it out. He does not need us to improve on it.

I believe the refusal to talk publicly about Jesus is the very core of America's problem.

You see, our founding fathers arrived under the power of the Lord Jesus Christ and were not ashamed to name Him. They rooted this republic in the belief that "there is neither Jew nor Greek, slave nor free, male nor female, for you are all one in Christ Jesus" (Gal. 3:28 NIV). And convinced of this equality in Christ, they flung wide America's doors for people like me to come in and share the nation's blessings.

What they never intended was that newcomers or succeeding generations would start to rearrange the furniture—to weaken the state by disowning its foundations. Sadly, our generation is, for the most part, ignorant of our foundation on the Solid Rock. Yet if you study the actual writings and documents of early American history, you will plainly see the imprint of the gospel of Jesus Christ.

For example, some 150 years before the adoption of the U.S. Constitution, the first written constitution in history was produced in Connecticut. It opens with these words:

> Forasmuch as it has pleased the Almighty God by the wise disposition of his divine providence so to order and dispose of things that we . . . are now . . . dwelling in and upon the River of Conectecotte . . . and well knowing where a people are gathered together the word of God requires that to maintain the peace and union of such a people there should be an orderly and decent government established according to God . . . [we] do therefore . . . enter into combination and confederation together, *to maintain and preserve the liberty and purity of the gospel of our Lord Jesus which we now profess,* as also the discipline of the Churches, which according to the truth of the said gospel is now practiced amongst us . . .

How much plainer could it be? Our constitutional form of government was intended "to maintain and preserve the liberty and purity of the gospel" of Jesus Christ. Our founding fathers named Him as Lord. Make no mistake: the days of American democracy will be numbered unless leaders and people once again acknowledge the power of Jesus' name.

Yet that is exactly what our modern, self-sufficient, secular culture cannot handle. People feel comfortable talking about God, but not Jesus. "God" is a kind of common ground where Muslims, Hindus, Buddhists, and New Agers can come together and kid themselves that they all believe in the same thing.

It is frightening how often this nebulous "God" is invoked at prayer breakfasts, just so people from other religions will feel at home. One of the reasons we still have the words *In God We Trust* on our dollar bills is that "God" can mean pretty much anything you want it to. Imagine the outcry if the Senate voted to replace *God* with *Jesus* on the national currency.

That's how far America has drifted from her moorings.

But the founding fathers were not Hindus or Buddhists or New Agers. And they certainly were not agnostics or atheists. They believed in Jesus Christ. They knew that, without Jesus, their faith wasn't worth half a hallelujah.

Study the Father's Portrait

Let's turn now to what Jesus taught us about His Father. For He painted a magnificent portrait in Luke 15, and, as with any great picture, the more we look at it, the more we see.

> There was a man who had two sons. The younger one said to his father, "Father, give me my share of the estate." So he divided his property between them.
>
> Not long after that, the younger son got together all he had, set off for a distant country and there squandered his wealth in wild living.

After he had spent everything, there was a severe famine in that whole country, and he began to be in need. So he went and hired himself out to a citizen of that country, who sent him to his fields to feed pigs. He longed to fill his stomach with the pods that the pigs were eating, but no one gave him anything.

When he came to his senses, he said, "How many of my father's hired men have food to spare, and here I am starving to death! I will set out and go back to my father and say to him: Father, I have sinned against heaven and against you. I am no longer worthy to be called your son; make me like one of your hired men." So he got up and went to his father.

But while he was still a long way off, his father saw him and was filled with compassion for him; he ran to his son, threw his arms around him and kissed him.

The son said to him, "Father, I have sinned against heaven and against you. I am no longer worthy to be called your son."

But the father said to his servants, "Quick! Bring the best robe and put it on him. Put a ring on his finger and sandals on his feet. Bring the fattened calf and kill it. Let's have a feast and celebrate. For this son of mine was dead and is alive again; he was lost and is found." So they began to celebrate.

Meanwhile, the older son was in the field. When he came near the house, he heard music and dancing. So he called one of the servants and asked him what was going on. "Your brother has come," he replied, "and your father has killed the fattened calf because he has him back safe and sound."

The older brother became angry and refused to go in. So his father went out and pleaded with him. But he answered his father, "Look! All these years I've been slaving for you and never disobeyed your orders. Yet you never gave me even a young goat so I could celebrate with my friends. But when this son of yours who has squandered your property with prostitutes comes home, you kill the fattened calf for him!"

"My son," the father said, "you are always with me, and everything I have is yours. But we had to celebrate and be glad, because this brother of yours was dead and is alive again; he was lost and is found." (Luke 15:11–32 NIV)

Immediately this portrait reveals certain things about the Father. The character of God unmistakably shines through. The father of the prodigal son is loving. He is caring. He is compassionate. He is patient. He is longsuffering. He is slow to anger. He is quick to forgive.

But notice also what the prodigal's father *did not do.*

What would your reaction be if your teenage son came to you one day and demanded that you liquidize his share of the family inheritance? I think you would give him pretty short shrift. Yet when the prodigal decided to leave home in rebellion, the father placed no obstacles in his way. In modern language, he "respected the boy's decision."

Can you imagine the hurt, the heartbreak he would have felt? Yet he quietly stood aside. When the boy left, the father resisted the temptation to mount a rescue mission. He sent no private detectives after him, made no attempt to influence his thinking, did nothing to save him from the pigs.

Was this negligence?

Not at all. The father longed for his son to come back. But he did not bend the rules of forgiveness to make it happen. Had he pursued the boy, had he gone out and assured him of forgiveness in order to bring him home, there would have been no repentance. Forgiveness would have had no meaning.

The son could not be restored to his father until he first realized his own desperate need of help. Only when he turned around and deliberately trudged back to the farm could he experience his father's love, forgiveness, and blessing.

If the prodigal had changed his mind again at the last minute, then he might as well have stayed with the pigs. If he had sent someone else to plead on his behalf, then he might as well have stayed with the pigs. He had to come back the father's way—and come the whole distance.

What It Means to Be the Prodigal Son

As you study this story, consider its implications.

Just like the prodigal, we have to return to God. We have to acknowledge our need and accept His terms. No great shows of repentance and remorse will bring about our salvation. We can blubber in the pigpen all we want; nothing will change until we get up and walk back home to put things right with God. For every one of us has broken our relationship with the Father. We have all demanded our share of His wealth and run off to squander it. And we must all take the same route back.

What can we expect when we come back to the Father? Again, let's look at the prodigal son. What happened is not what we would anticipate.

When the boy finally comes home, he knows he is in disgrace. Everyone would expect the father to remain aloof while the boy makes his way through the village. The son would then be obliged to sit outside the gate for some time while the doorman asks the father if he will let him in. After a considerable time had passed, the son would be summoned.

Punishment of some kind would be inevitable. The village would be led to understand that the father had indeed preserved the family honor through discipline. The father would be very angry, and the boy would have to publicly apologize for dishonoring his father's name.

But none of that happens.

The father of the prodigal son reacts in a most unvillagelike manner: he goes running down the road to meet his son. The word used in Scripture here does not mean a slow shuffle; it means he *raced* down the road. He could not get to his son fast enough.

If you have spent any time in the Middle East, you will understand what a very unusual occurrence this was. In that culture, men over thirty never run. They always walk slowly and with dignity; that is considered proper for their position and stature in the community.

Some years ago I was traveling in the Middle East, and I called a friend to ask where would be a good place to run, so I could get some exercise.

He bellowed on the other side of the phone. "What? You must not let anybody see you! It is not dignified to be seen running."

Yet the prodigal's father ran. It was the compassion of his heart that led him to do what is normally not done for a rebellious boy. The father ran so that he would take upon himself the shame and the humiliation that the boy would normally face in society.

Can you capture here the mystery and wonder of God in Christ?

What It Means to Be the Older Brother

At this point you may be thinking, "Well, I've repented already; I'm in God's family. What has all this to do with me?"

If so, watch out! For there are *two* children in Jesus' portrait of the Father. We have all been the prodigal. Now let's be careful not to turn into the self-satisfied older brother.

The prodigal never expected to be restored to the family ("Treat me as one of your hired servants!" he said). For his older brother, though, family life had become so routine that he no longer saw its opportunities and potentials. Christians who resemble the older brother do all the right things. They sing in the choir, read all the latest Christian books, listen to all the popular teaching tapes. And somehow in the midst of all this they get walled off from their heavenly Father. All their energy and attention goes into their work for God. And in their hearts, just like the older brother, they "refuse to go in" to the place where God really is.

What happens if we become like the older brother? Hidden behind this attitude is a spiritual pride that prevents us from enjoying all the benefits of life in God's family. It stops our knowing God as Father. It makes us too conscious of our own intellect to call God "Daddy." It gives us such a regard for our own opinion that we never seek God's help as Guide and Mentor.

If you have this kind of pride, I pray to God that you will give it up.

Because the pathology of pride is this: it makes you try to earn what already belongs to you by right. Unable to accept the gifts that the heavenly Father loves to bestow on His children, pride tries to make you independent, to make you stand aloof, or to make you believe that the blessings you receive are less than you deserve.

Many have seen the older brother as a reference to the Jewish people. This is true insofar as his attitude is a type of the resentment of the Jewish people—accustomed to being God's chosen people—at the message of the gospel: that Gentiles could inherit the kingdom of God through faith in Christ. But at a deeper level the older brother represents a sterile religiosity as common today as it was among the Pharisees.

In the modern world, the "older brother" is far more likely to be:

- a regular churchgoer

- a person who wants to believe in God his or her own way

- a person who puts great store in being righteous and moral

- a person who seldom admits to error

- a person who cannot accept forgiveness through the shed blood of Jesus Christ at Calvary

Understand this: the father in Jesus' portrait loved both his sons. God our Father loves those who have "stayed" as much as those who have "strayed." His heart is broken alike by willful rebellion and by stubborn ingratitude. And He reaches out to both sorts of individuals. There is nothing you can do to make God love you more. There is nothing you can do to make God love you less. He loves you, and nothing is going to make Him stop.

In the end, that little phrase "Our Father" reduces all of life's complications to something very simple. Can you honestly begin to pray with those words? Can you turn to God and say, "Our Father"? If you can't, it's time to turn things around.

Finally, let's look briefly at the way God does His parenting.

Four Things God's Fatherhood Means

We have a problem with fatherhood in America. We have made fathers and mothers the same, and destroyed the identities of both. But when Jesus told us to pray "Our Father," He was not thinking of "Mr. Mom."

Jesus' contemporaries understood some basics about fatherhood that our culture is trying to forget. They knew that a father was a provider, protector, and director for his family.

I thank God for the way women pick up the broken pieces in the wake of irresponsible men. I thank God especially for single mothers, and pray God will give them a double portion of His blessing. But that only underlines the fact that fathers have a job to do in the family—and they need to come to terms with it.

God's parenting class gives us the lead. The Father provides four things for His children, and as human fathers we should provide the same things—on a smaller scale—for ours.

1. Freedom from fear. Having God for my Father spells an end to all my fears. In many religions, gods and ancestral spirits create terror. They are capricious, bad-tempered, and uncontrollable. But I am not afraid of my God. In fact, I am not afraid at all, period. For my heavenly Father loves me, and I know that with Him all things—whether I understand them or not—will turn out for good.

2. Confidence. My heavenly Father gives me all the hope and the confidence I need, and banishes my uncertainty. Because He loves me, I know who I am. I know what my life's mission is. I know what He expects of me, and what my reward will be when this earthly life is over. My Father in heaven gives me protection, safety, security, serenity, salvation, and peace. And in this confidence I have joy, even when life causes me pain.

3. Companionship. There are no latchkey kids in the household of God. My heavenly Father is never too busy to spend time with me. His

support and friendship are with me in hardships and temptations. Human families and friends may let me down, but my heavenly Daddy has promised never to leave me or forsake me. Jesus said in John 14, "Whoever has my commands and obeys them, he is the one who loves me. He who loves me will be loved by my Father, and I too will love him and show myself to him" (v. 21 NIV).

4. **Provision.** Human fathers work to feed and clothe their families. Our heavenly Father does much more. All the resources of heaven are available to God's children. The problem is that we do not trust Him to be our heavenly supplier. Yet didn't Jesus tell us that God gives good things to those who ask Him? When you pray for bread, God does not give you a stone.

Yet if we're not careful, we can hinder our heavenly Father's provision for our needs.

LET GO OF THOSE BLESSINGS

As a pastor I frequently encounter individuals who are not experiencing the fullness of the Father's provision.

Recently, for example, when share prices were plunging, a man who invests heavily said to me, "Oh, isn't it terrible what is happening to the stock market?" He was worried and moaning.

I knew the wealthy man was a tightwad who sought God only in an economic downturn; prayer was his panic button. And he was not a giver. My answer was, "Let me ask you this. What did you do for God when the stock market was up?"

He looked at me blankly.

But the fact is, in God's family the relationships run two ways. God has an unlimited supply of blessings for His children. But we have to learn to give as well as take.

Even the worst parents know you do not help children by continually showering them with gifts. The objective of parenthood is to raise strong, good, dependable kids. And that means you have to give them discipline.

So it is with God. When things go wrong we should ask ourselves, "Have I used my blessings as God would wish?"

Something you learn pretty fast in the Christian faith is that you can hold only so many blessings in your hands. If you want more blessings tomorrow, you will have to give away the ones God gave you yesterday. We give—and then we receive. If we don't give, we block the opportunity for God to pour out His resources.

The first lesson about prayer, then, is to start where you should be— as a child of God who has the right and the privilege to say the words "Our Father."

The second lesson is about where we are going, and where God already is: heaven. We'll talk about that in Chapter 3.

PRAYER WORKBOOK

TO REFLECT ON:

As a starting point, think about your earthly parents. Not everybody has happy memories of childhood. Whether your memories are positive or negative, write down two things you have appreciated about the way your father brought you up—things you might like to thank him for. I have written down two things I appreciated about my father. Put your answers in the spaces that follow.

MY ANSWERS

1. He had very high standards; I always knew what he expected of me.
2. He set a good example in self-discipline.

YOUR ANSWERS

1. _____

_____

2. _____

_____

As we grow up, our relationship with our earthly parents changes. We begin to know them as adults and equals, and eventually they die and we have to get along without them. But with God we do not "grow up" in the same way. He never leaves us. We remain His children for eternity. Look at the two things you have appreciated about your earthly father, and ask yourself how these reflect qualities in your heavenly Father.

MY ANSWERS

1. Through His Word my heavenly Father has given me a clear picture of the way He wants me to live.
2. In Jesus I have the perfect example of how I should order my life and handle my relationships.

YOUR ANSWERS

1. _____

2. _____
   _____

TO READ:
Spend a few minutes quietly reflecting on these Scriptures:

Then little children were brought to Jesus for him to place his hands on them and pray for them. But the disciples rebuked those who brought them.

Jesus said, "Let the little children come to me, and do not hinder them, for the kingdom of heaven belongs to such as these." (Matt. 19:13–15 NIV)

While Jesus was still talking to the crowd, his mother and brothers stood outside, wanting to speak to him. Someone told him, "Your mother and brothers are standing outside, wanting to speak to you."

He replied, "Who is my mother, and who are my brothers?" Pointing to his disciples, he said, "Here are my mother and my brothers.

For whoever does the will of my Father in heaven is my brother and sister and mother." (Matt. 12:46–50 NIV)

So he got up and went to his father.

But while he was still a long way off, his father saw him and was filled with compassion for him; he ran to his son, threw his arms around him and kissed him.

The son said to him "Father, I have sinned against heaven and against you. I am no longer worthy to be called your son."

But the father said to his servants, "Quick! Bring the best robe and put it on him. Put a ring on his finger and sandals on his feet. Bring the fattened calf and kill it. Let's have a feast and celebrate. For this son of mine was dead and is alive again; he was lost and is found." (Luke 15:20–24 NIV)

TO PRAY:

Finally, take a legal pad. Collect all your thoughts and write a prayer that expresses how you feel about your heavenly Father. Try to avoid using "stock phrases." Make sure that everything you thank God for, and everything you ask Him for, comes from your heart and has meaning for you personally. Make the prayer as long or as short as you wish. When you are satisfied with it, copy it into this book. Then spend a little time quietly in the presence of your heavenly Father before speaking it out loud.

This is my prayer. Write yours in the space that follows.

MY PRAYER

I am thankful I can call You Father. There were many things I could not tell my earthly father when he was alive—the generation gap separated us, and I was afraid he would not understand. But You, my heavenly Father, understand everything, You know everything, You see everything. I have no secrets to hide from You.

Father, You are firm and just. Yet You are also tender-hearted, merciful, and understanding. Whenever I come into Your presence, You are always available. Though many earthly fathers are too busy to spend time with their children, You are always there ready to hear me . . . what a privilege! May You never permit me to take this privilege—or You—for granted.

You are a kind Father.

You are a generous Father.

You are a gracious Father.

You are a loving Father.

Your love is infinitely more than the best of a father's love. May I, today, be Your kind of a father to my children. May I, today, be the kind of a father You want me to be. Gentle but firm. Kind but strong. Meek yet humble. Generous yet wise. Giving only good gifts that are glorifying to Your name and to the name of my older brother, the Lord Jesus.

Above all, help me today to recognize that in the kingdom of God I am not a father at all—only Your child.

YOUR PRAYER

"In Heaven"

3

Know Where You're Going

Like millions of people before me, I came to America to discover a new life.

It has now been twenty-three years since I stepped off the plane in Los Angeles, but I can remember clearly the hours Elizabeth and I spent poring over books and magazines, searching out every detail we could find about the nation that would be our home.

We laughed as we studied a map of Pasadena, California, searching in vain for a body of water anywhere near Lake Avenue. Why else would it be named Lake Avenue if there were no lake? But there wasn't. It didn't make sense.

But everything about our new country was different—the currency, climate, housing, transportation, schooling, medicine, business and political freedoms—and everything was exciting.

HAVE HEAVEN ON YOUR MIND

You would expect most Christians to think about heaven the way Elizabeth and I thought about the United States. With excitement. With eager anticipation.

After all, no one makes a major investment then never bothers to check how that investment is doing. No one buys a train ticket then rolls out a sleeping bag and stays at the station. Yet that is pretty much the kind of shortsightedness Christians display about eternal life.

Ask yourself this question. When did you last give any serious thought to heaven? A month ago? Twelve months ago? The fact is, Christians seldom give heaven the time of day. Still less do we make any proper preparations for going there.

Most of us pretend we are going to live this life forever. All our attention and energy goes into planning our short-term future on earth. We will spend hours choosing a place to go for our next two-week vacation. But ask what plans someone has for their eternal stay in heaven, and most people will stare at you blankly. It has never crossed their minds.

Now, it's true that earthly business can be very pressing. And it is possible—as the saying goes—to be "so heavenly minded as to be of no earthly use." Yet our final entry into heaven is among the basics of Christian belief. You are headed for heaven by the assurance of the shed blood of Jesus Christ on Calvary. If you put your faith in Christ, and your sins are forgiven, then you already have a ticket in your hand that says HEAVEN—ADMIT ONE.

We need to rediscover the attitude shown by Sir Thomas More. At the height of his career as chancellor under England's Henry VIII, More wrote a letter to a friend saying how much he wanted to retire. What was behind it? Did he want to get out on the golf links and perfect his swing? Nothing like that. What he longed for, he said, was time to "contemplate the afterlife."

Like More, we should recognize the importance of the place we're going. And we should spend some of our precious time reading the "travel brochures" and preparing to live there. Don't know where to begin? Then let me introduce you to someone who visited heaven while he was still on earth: the apostle Paul.

HEAVEN—A TRAVEL GUIDE

In his second letter to the Corinthians, Paul supplies one of the Bible's few eyewitness accounts of heaven. The revelation of heaven made quite an impact on him: "I know a man in Christ who fourteen years ago was caught up to the third heaven . . . And I know that this man—whether in the body or apart from the body I do not know, but God knows—was caught up to Paradise. He heard inexpressible things, things that man is not permitted to tell" (2 Cor. 12:2–4 NIV).

We all know people who brag about the exotic destinations they have been to. But Paul was not bragging; he was laying out his credentials as an apostle. Because he did not want to sound boastful about his experience, he wrote about it in the third person: "I know a man." Paul, of course, was that man.

What did Paul say heaven was like? He did not give any details, perhaps because God did not permit him to tell about it in depth. But he heard "inexpressible things"— things that really could not be put into words. Human language would have been inadequate to describe it. What comes across most strongly in Paul's description is his own sense of speechless wonder. It is like hearing someone recall a dream.

Yet heaven is no dream. From Genesis to Revelation, the Bible uses the word *heaven* to denote three distinct but definitely *physical* locations.

1. **The atmosphere.** When Isaiah 55:10 says that the rain comes "down from heaven," we should not imagine angels pouring buckets of water over the parapets of the heavenly city. Isaiah uses *heaven* to mean "the place where the clouds are."

2. **Outer space.** In other parts of Scripture, *heaven* denotes the sun, moon, and stars—everything in the realm of the constellations. Speaking of this, Psalm 19:1 tells us that "the heavens declare the glory of God" (NIV)—in other words, that their majesty commends His handiwork.

3. **The home of God.** This is what Paul refers to as the "third heaven" in his letter to the Corinthians. It is God's special place, the part of the universe where His rule goes unchallenged. The Bible clearly speaks of it as a country, with a city—the New Jerusalem—at its center. One day that heavenly city will descend to earth, as Revelation foretells (21:2). Meanwhile, Jesus goes around His Father's house, making sure the rooms are ready for us to move into (John 14:2–3).

Occasionally people wonder how God can be "in heaven" and also be omnipresent. A Sunday school teacher once put the problem to his class of nine-year-olds—and got the answer he deserved when a little girl replied, "Silly, heaven is just His headquarters."

Children can be so wise. God controls all three heavens. He is the power that sustains the atmosphere, the cosmos, and the heavenly country. Yet, incredibly, this vast and transcendent God also occupies the believer's heart.

It is a paradox. You will never be able to explain it to someone whose spiritual eyes are closed, for outside the realm of faith it makes no sense. Nevertheless, the same Father whose headquarters are in heaven, whose hand holds together the spinning galaxies, also comforts us, blesses us, and speaks peace to the troubled soul. Even as we pray "Our Father in heaven," our heavenly Father is nearer to us than our own hands and feet.

HOW BADLY DO YOU WANT TO GET THERE?

So heaven is a place. Yet the things that make heaven amazing cannot be reduced to a list of tourist attractions. No doubt the accommodations will surpass the finest hotels on earth, but we will not be going out in the morning with a Berlitz travel guide to ogle at the golden pavements. Heaven is not Las Vegas.

Listen again to Paul, who was writing this time to the Philippian church. So intensely did he long to be in heaven that he continued his earthly ministry only from a sense of duty. He confessed, "I am hard-pressed between the two . . . my desire is to depart and be in heaven with Christ for that is much better . . . but to remain in the flesh is more necessary for your sake" (Phil. 1:23–24 author's translation).

Paul—who had seen heaven firsthand—could not wait to get there. He longed for it. And his hunger for heaven is one every Christian should share. After all, "our citizenship is in heaven" (Phil. 3:20 NIV).

That verse in Philippians means a lot to me, because I know what it is to be a naturalized citizen in an adopted country. In 1984 I became a U.S. citizen, having immigrated here in 1977. I relinquished my citizenship in the country of my birth, Egypt, and became a citizen of a different country. I have a deep and abiding affection for my adopted country and consider myself privileged to be able to choose to live here. But as much as I love America, it does not hold the attraction for me that heaven does—because that is where my ultimate citizenship lies.

I became a "naturalized" citizen of heaven when I entered a relationship with Jesus Christ and became a partaker of His divine nature. As believers, we have been adopted into God's family and granted citizenship in an adopted country—heaven—the eternal dwelling place of Almighty God, our Father.

The glimpses and foretastes of heaven supplied to us in the Bible should whet our appetites and make us long to depart this world and be with Him in heaven.

Examine your heart. Heaven should be the fulfillment of your greatest spiritual longings. In fact—let me be frank—if you're having such a great time down here that heaven can wait, there may be something wrong with your salvation. If you never hunger for heaven, you should take a long, hard look at your walk with the Lord.

Let me show you what I mean.

HEAVEN HAS NO SNAILS

A fable tells of a beautiful swan alighting on the banks of a river where a crane was wading in search of snails. The crane had never seen a swan before. "Where did you come from?" the crane said, blinking stupidly.

"I came from heaven," replied the swan.

"What is heaven?"

The swan could not believe it. "You've never heard of heaven?" So the beautiful bird went on to describe the grandeur of the eternal city, the walls made of precious stone, the crystal-pure river of life and the tree whose leaves heal the nations.

All this, however, aroused not the slightest interest on the part of the crane.

Finally the crane asked, "Are there any snails there?"

"Snails?" replied the swan. "No, of course there are no snails there."

"Then," said the crane, as it went back to wading through the slime, "you can have your heaven. Personally, I prefer snails."

This fable contains a deep truth.

Earthly life is much concerned with snails. Some people catch a lot of fat snails and feel very pleased with themselves. Others dredge up only a few small ones. Either way, success and happiness are measured on the same, limited scale.

It follows that people whose lives revolve around snails—by which, of course, I mean worldly ideas of the "good life"—will tend to see heaven as a place where desires are gratified. To them, heaven means health, wealth, and happiness—all the things they would like more of on earth.

That being so, we should not be surprised at the results of a 1991 Gallup poll. This showed that 78 percent of Americans expect to go to heaven when they die. It also revealed that many of those responding never pray, never read the Bible, and never attend a church. In fact, most of them admitted that their prime concern was to please themselves first.

Which leads to a difficult question: If these sorts of people actually made it into heaven, *would they enjoy it?*

Imagine their situation. They have rejected Jesus Christ as their only

Savior. Throughout their lives they have kept God at arm's length. And now they want to come to the one place they cannot escape Him. Would they really be happy? Surely, for someone who wanted nothing to do with God, heaven would be a kind of hell! The whole idea is absurd.

No, there are no snails in heaven. Heaven is amazing—is truly heaven and not hell—because it supplies in full measure the things the spirit longs for, not the things the flesh craves. Whatever it was Paul saw on his visit to paradise, you can bet your bottom dollar it was not sundecks and swimming pools. Heaven offers far greater prizes than that—prizes so great and valuable we can barely begin to imagine them.

Let's look briefly at nine biblical reasons why Christians should want to go to heaven. For these are the things that tell us what heaven is really like.

THE NINE BENEFITS OF HEAVEN

1. **No more temptation.** Once we get to heaven, we will be free from Satan's assaults. We will no longer struggle against the pressure of temptation. There will be no more deceptions or fiery darts. Satan will no longer be able to damage our relationships with each other by feeding suspicion, resentment, and misunderstanding.

2. **No more loss.** Our lives on earth are blighted by change and loss. The people we love are taken away from us. Again and again we encounter partings of the way and suffer heart-wrenching separations. But not in heaven. To arrive in heaven is to come home. We will live in unity and community. The keynote of our existence will be quiet contentment. Restlessness, anxiety, bereavement—all these will be left behind.

3. **No more tears.** C. S. Lewis wrote in *The Problem of Pain*: "Life carries with it more pain than pleasure for many of God's children . . . the most bitter tears are those shed inwardly or alone when no one else sees the agony of our spirits." But in heaven all tears will be wiped away.

For heaven spells an end to bitterness and frustration. To live in the fullness of God's presence is to know that all your hopes can be realized.

4. **No more death.** On earth, death always lies in the future. Even Christians can be overshadowed by it. But we should not be infected by the secular world's fear of dying. For death is not an end to life; it's moving from one house to another. It's a door, a passport control desk, an escalator to another level. And once you are in heaven, death vanishes into the past. It no longer has any power over you. You are home and free from all dangers.

5. **No more regrets.** How often have you looked back and said, "I wish I had never said that"? On earth our words and actions have consequences we cannot control. A whole line of dominoes goes tumbling down, and we are powerless to set them up again. Not so in heaven. Arriving there we turn the last page on all our unkind words and selfish deeds. In Christ they are gone, expunged, wiped away. We start over.

6. **No more separation.** As Paul wrote, "Now we see but a poor reflection; then we shall see face to face" (1 Cor. 13:12 NIV). On earth the pressures of life quickly distract us. We need churches and sanctuaries—special havens that let us enter God's presence and remember how magnificent He is. But there will be no church building programs in heaven. Nor, for that matter, any separation between church and state. We will sense God's presence fully, everywhere we go, and in everything we do.

7. **No more schedules.** I'm serious! The Bible tells us that in heaven God will dispense with the sun and moon, and thus free us from our enslavement to time. We will not be forever meeting deadlines and dashing for appointments. No longer will we have to negotiate the endless cycles of days and seasons. Instead, we will live an unhurried life. There will be time for everything—and no excuse for a double booking.

8. **No more darkness.** Not only will God banish the darkness of night, but He will also banish the darkness of misunderstanding. He will

remove the darkness of anger and hurt. So much of the time other people's behavior mystifies us. Often we mystify ourselves. We struggle to plumb the depths of our motivation and to understand why we do what we do. But not in heaven. There, as Paul said, "I shall know fully, even as I am fully known" (1 Cor. 13:12 NIV).

9. No more disillusionment. One of the defining qualities of earthly life is meaninglessness; if you don't believe that, just read the book of Ecclesiastes! Our best efforts and loftiest achievements can leave us disappointed and disenchanted. Mountaintop "highs" can give way to months in the valleys. But heaven gets us off the treadmill. Life will no longer seem empty or wasted, for we will be busy reigning and ruling with God.

WHAT ABOUT THE PEOPLE WHO AREN'T THERE?

A rather subtle argument against heaven goes like this: how can heaven be heaven for Christians when they know that some of their loved ones have been left outside?

We need to take this seriously. After all, human beings are prone to comfort one another in bereavement by saying that "everyone goes to heaven," and that, as a result, the separation is only temporary.

Fortunately, children are less mealy-mouthed about it.

After the death of the family cat, a mother trotted out the old line by telling the kids, "Don't worry, Toby is in heaven now." Her daughter promptly replied, "But, Mom . . . what would God want with a dead cat?"

I have some news for pet lovers. Pets do not have souls; they don't go to heaven. When they die, you aren't going to see them again.

But exactly the same issue arises when people die. In fact, not long ago a member of my congregation confronted me with a similar question: "What if we get to heaven and realize that some of our loved ones are not there? What will happen?"

I believe the Bible gives us two answers.

First, if you have a family member who is not a believer, it is God's will and desire for that person to come to Him. God is a covenant-making God, and He makes covenants with families. So if God brings one person from a family into the kingdom, He desires the whole family to follow. Never give up praying for your unsaved father or mother, husband or wife, brother or sister, or son or daughter. God wants them to be with you.

But second, don't forget that in heaven we will not have the same emotional ties we feel so strongly down here. On earth the loyalties and attachments we form by being close to others move us very powerfully. But arriving in heaven will feel a little like waking from a dream. We will enter a new and higher reality, and from that new vantage point we will understand justice, love, grace, and mercy with a perfection we cannot begin to grasp from where we are now.

HEAVEN TODAY!

Many churches hear the Lord's Prayer read Sunday after Sunday, without giving a second thought to heaven. One little boy had been reciting "Our Father who art in Heaven" for six whole months at Sunday school before he confounded his mother by asking, "Mom, who is Art, and why is he in heaven?"

Which raises a last and vitally important point. Yes, heaven is a real place where all believers will one day go. But it is also a present reality in our hearts. When you invite Jesus into your life, He brings a foretaste of heaven with Him. As He said in Luke 17:20 NIV, "The kingdom of God is within you."

Most Christians think it is their present life that's real and concrete, and that the kingdom of heaven can safely be left till later. Actually, it's the other way around. Life on this earth is slipping past and fading away; what matters most is to invest in the heavenly home you're going to. It's a bit like a savings plan. How much you invest now determines how much you get back later.

Let me illustrate.

A farmer took the new country preacher to his property and stood with him on a small hill next to the homestead.

Pointing to the north, he said to the preacher, "As far as your eye can see in this direction, I own." Then he turned to the west and said, "As far as your eye can see in that direction, I own." Then he turned again, to the south, and then to the east, and said the same thing: "As far as your eye can see in that direction, I own."

At first the young preacher was taken aback. But then he looked the farmer in the eye and said, "Let me ask you this." Then he pointed heavenward and said, "How much do you own in *that* direction?"

You may wonder, "Can I own things in heaven?" You'd better believe it! In 1 Timothy 6 the apostle Paul told Timothy that Christians should do good, be generous, and share. "In this way they will lay up treasure for themselves as a firm foundation for the coming age, so that they may take hold of the life that is truly life" (v. 19 NIV).

So take stock. Pull your eyes off your current financial situation and look upward—for your real home, and your real interests, lie with your Father in heaven.

How much do you own in that direction?

PRAYER WORKBOOK

TO REFLECT ON:

As a starting point, think about a place you have loved—perhaps your childhood home, or a place you went on vacation that brings you happy memories. Write down two things you really liked about that place, reasons why it is special to you. I have written down two things I enjoyed about a place I have visited just outside of Tuscany, Italy. Put your answers in the spaces that follow.

MY ANSWERS

1. It is a mountain area of great natural beauty.
2. It is remote and peaceful, removed from the worries and pressures of everyday life.

YOUR ANSWERS

1. _____
   _____
2. _____
   _____

Heaven will be different from anything we have experienced on earth. It is really a false comparison to consider heaven in terms of earthly places, yet the joys we associate with particular places in some way foreshadow heaven. Think about the place you chose in your last answer. Do your memories of it give you any clues as to what you look forward to in heaven? Write down two things you think will be special about heaven, and that make you happy you are going to be there.

MY ANSWERS

1. Heaven is not a place of natural beauty but supernatural splendor, illuminated by Jesus Himself.
2. Heaven will be a place of perfect peace with none of the cares of life that frustrate us.

YOUR ANSWERS

1. _____
_____
2. _____
_____

TO READ:

Spend a few minutes quietly reflecting on these Scriptures:

Now we know that if the earthly tent we live in is destroyed, we have a building from God, an eternal house in heaven, not built by human hands. Meanwhile we groan, longing to be clothed with our heavenly dwelling, because when we are clothed, we will not be found naked. For while we are in this tent, we groan and are burdened, because we do not wish to be unclothed but to be clothed with our heavenly dwelling, so that what is mortal may be swallowed up by life. (2 Cor. 5:1–4 NIV)

He called a little child and had him stand among them. And he said: "I tell you the truth, unless you change and become like little children, you will never enter the kingdom of heaven. Therefore, whoever humbles himself like this child is the greatest in the kingdom of heaven. And whoever welcomes a little child like this in my name welcomes me." (Matt. 18:2–5 NIV)

I saw the Holy City, the new Jerusalem, coming down out of heaven from God, prepared as a bride beautifully dressed for her husband. And I heard a loud voice from the throne saying, "Now the dwelling of God is with men, and he will live with them. They will be his people, and God himself will be with them and be their God. He will wipe every tear from their eyes. There will be no more death or mourning or crying or pain, for the old order of things has passed away . . .

[The Holy City] shone with the glory of God, and its brilliance was like that of a very precious jewel, like a jasper, clear as crystal. It had a great, high wall with twelve gates, and with twelve angels at the gates . . .

The wall was made of jasper, and the city of pure gold, as pure as glass. The foundations of the city walls were decorated with every kind of precious stone. The first foundation was jasper, the second sapphire, the third chalcedony, the fourth emerald, the fifth sardonyx, the sixth carnelian, the seventh chrysolite, the eighth beryl, the ninth topaz, the tenth chrysoprase, the eleventh jacinth, and the twelfth amethyst. The twelve gates were twelve pearls, each gate made of a single pearl. The street of the city was of pure gold, like transparent glass.

I did not see a temple in the city, because the Lord God Almighty and the Lamb are its temple. The city does not need the sun or the moon to shine on it, for the glory of God gives it light, and the Lamb is its lamp. The nations will walk by its light, and the kings of the earth will bring their splendor into it. On no day will its gates ever be shut, for there will be no night there. (Rev. 21:2–4, 11–12, 18–25 NIV)

TO PRAY:

Finally, take a legal pad. Collect all your thoughts and write a prayer that expresses how you feel about heaven. As before, try to avoid using "stock phrases." Make sure that everything you thank God for, and everything you ask Him for, comes from your heart and has meaning for you personally. Make the prayer as long or as short as you wish. When you are satisfied with it, copy it into this book. Then spend a little time quietly in the presence of your heavenly Father before speaking it out loud. This is my prayer. Write yours in the space that follows.

MY PRAYER

Father, while You are with me here and now, You are also in Your dwelling places in universes I cannot comprehend.

Though You are everywhere at once, Your Word also tells me that there is a place called heaven. There the multitudes of angels and the saints who have gone before us constantly praise Your holy and majestic name.

In heaven there is no sorrow or pain.

In heaven there is no sin or rebellion.

In heaven there is only complete and perfect peace.

Thank You that one day I will be with You because of what Jesus did on the cross for me. As a Christian believer I can have that assurance of heaven.

Heaven is Your headquarters. It is from heaven that You rule these vast universes with a precision that eludes humanity's greatest minds.

The more scientists try to comprehend the vastness of Your universe, the more they realize that they are but children playing in the sand next to a cosmic ocean.

People may say that things are out of control. They may fear for the future of our planet. Yet You are in perfect control of every galaxy in the universe.

With all of Your unfathomable greatness, and in the midst of this spectacular universe, You have created my tiny being and invited me to call You "my Father in heaven."

Today may I bring a little bit of heaven to someone who is hurting or lonely. Today may I remember, and be ready to remind others, that heaven is my real home.

No matter how many years You bless me with, in the end I will be coming home.

May I look forward to heaven.

May heaven motivate my life's activities.

May heaven be the place where I put my treasure, my heart, and my hope.

YOUR PRAYER

_____

_____

_____

_____

_____

_____

_____

_____

_____

_____

_____

_____

_____

_____

_____

_____

_____

_____

_____

_____

_____

"Hallowed Be Your Name"

4

Exalting God's Name

Soon after I was conceived, three different doctors advised my mother to get an abortion.

They all reached the same conclusion: "You have had six children already, and three miscarriages in the last seven years. You are just too weak; your health will not support another pregnancy. If you insist on having this child, you will almost certainly die."

For my mother, my birth meant a death sentence—at least according to the medical experts.

My parents were both faithful believers. They knew it was not God's will to take the life of an unborn child. Yet the risk to my mother's life was so great, the doctors had already scheduled the procedure. What an agonizing decision my parents faced: trying to carry this baby to term would most likely mean leaving their six other children motherless. They cried out to God.

And without a clear word from God in answer to their prayer, things might have turned out very differently.

God's answer to my parents came through their pastor, Ayad Girgis, a godly man who knew how to pray the prayer that God will answer. In a late-night visit just before the scheduled surgery, the pastor shared with my parents how he had been unable to sleep for several nights as he had sought God about their desperate situation.

"God is involved in this pregnancy," he said. "Do not be afraid. You will have the strength and health to raise this child, because this child will be born to serve the Lord."

Born to serve the Lord. It was the divine reassurance my parents needed to reach a courageous decision: they would do what they knew to be right and trust God to look after them. They canceled the abortion.

I am certainly glad they did!

But here's the point to note. So thankful were they for God's answer to prayer, that they gave me a special name: *Michael*.

NAMES HAVE MEANINGS

Lots of men are called Michael, and you may not think there is anything so very wonderful about it. But that's only because in the West we have ceased to think of names as significant.

It was William Shakespeare who asserted:

> What's in a name? That which we call a rose
> By any other name would smell as sweet.
> (Romeo and Juliet, II, ii)

From this perspective, it's what you *are* that matters—not what you're called. Names are arbitrary. They have no more effect on you than the filename has on a document you attach it to. You could call yourself anything you want, and you would still be the same person.

In fact, though, we do not use names in quite so cavalier a fashion. Many people in the West name their child after a favorite movie star, hoping (presumably) that a bit of the glamor will rub off. Others pick the name of a loved relative. One eager man in England gave his son the names of all eleven players on the national soccer team.

This idea that names say something about a person is deeply ingrained. After all, most of us think we know what sort of person a Tom is as opposed to a Harry or a Stanton. The whole tragedy in Shakespeare's *Romeo and Juliet*, quoted previously, is that the two young lovers belong to different families, with different names, and can never be allowed to marry.

Why do we choose names so carefully?

Well, one reason is we caught the habit from Scripture. Read the Old Testament and you will soon discover that names are as significant as their owners. A name not only represents a person, it explains who he is. More than that, it actually defines the role he will act out. Thus the successor to Moses, who led the people of Israel into the promised land, is called Joshua, meaning "Savior." Likewise Solomon, whose name means "peace," put an end to the feuding that followed the death of his father, King David.

Sometimes God changed people's names. When the child Isaac came along, Abram ("father of height") became Abraham ("father of a multitude"). Later, Isaac's son Jacob (the "supplanter" of his elder brother Esau) became Israel ("ruling with God").

To receive a name in the Bible was to have your destiny set in stone. Consequently, when my parents looked for a name to give me, they did not pick it out of a telephone directory or a Hollywood magazine. They wanted my name to remind everyone I was a miracle. For the name *Michael* means "who is like God."

WHAT DOES GOD'S NAME MEAN?

There is a story about a Mr. and Mrs. Brown who felt their family name lacked distinction and tried to compensate for it by calling their son Fantastic.

This was a mistake. As he grew up, Fantastic Brown came to hate his name with a vengeance. He cringed every time he heard it, and given the chance would gladly have changed it to Freddie, Frank, or even

Fernando. But in a small town, of course, everyone called him Fantastic whether he liked it or not, and he had to grin and bear it.

Shortly before he died, however, he determined that the hated name should not follow him into the grave. He told his wife, "I want to make one request. Don't put the name Fantastic on my tombstone. Just put Brown."

This left his wife in a quandary. On the one hand, her husband had been a wonderful man, and she wanted to honor his request. On the other hand, she'd loved the name Fantastic from the day she first saw him, and did not want to commemorate him as plain old Mr. Brown.

Finally she came up with a solution.

She had inscribed on his tombstone the following words:

BROWN
During his long marriage he never looked at another woman

Which worked perfectly—because everyone who walked past the tombstone gasped and said, "That's fantastic!"

I can't vouch for the story's authenticity. But I can empathize with poor Fantastic Brown, because I had a similar experience.

In the culture of Egypt in the 1940s and 1950s, family names possessed enormous importance. My numerous relatives all agreed that our family name was more precious than silver. It was a source of prestige and the basis of trust. If any of the Youssef boys were even suspected of keeping bad company, or of failing to be polite, or of illicitly puffing a cigarette, our father came down on us like a ton of bricks.

"You have brought disgrace on the good name of the family!" he would roar. "Our name matters more than money. It matters more than anything. Everybody sees what you do—it is your duty to uphold our honor!"

After I had heard this lecture a few dozen times, not surprisingly I grew to resent it. I had not asked to be given this priceless family name. It was foisted on me without my consent. If being a Youssef carried all this unwanted responsibility, I'd rather be called something else.

In both cases—Fantastic Brown's and my own—a gap opened up between the names we had been given and the people we were. Neither of us seemed to "fit the bill."

But there is one person who consistently lives up to His name. In fact, His name so fully expresses His character, reputation, authority, and power, that the ancient Israelites made almost no distinction between God's name and God Himself. They would not pronounce God's name, and when they wrote it down they deliberately left out the vowels, so that it appears only as YHWH.

God's name, then, does not have a meaning so much as it carries a power. It's like a lightning conductor. So when God appeared to Moses in the burning bush:

> Moses said to God, "Suppose I go to the Israelites and say to them, 'The God of your fathers has sent me to you,' and they ask me, 'What is his name?' Then what shall I tell them?"
>
> God said to Moses, "I am who I am. This is what you are to say to the Israelites: 'I AM has sent me to you.'"
>
> God also said to Moses, "Say to the Israelites, 'The Lord, the God of your fathers—the God of Abraham, the God of Isaac and the God of Jacob—has sent me to you.' This is my name for ever, the name by which I am to be remembered from generation to generation." (Ex. 3:13–15 NIV)

God instructed Moses to call Him "I AM." Not "I WAS" or "I WILL BE." He made it clear that He would be perpetually present in His name. While the generations of human beings come and go, God *is*. He does not change. He remains constant, in all His resplendence and power. And over a thousand years later, Jesus, who is God expressed in human form, drove this point home to the Pharisees:

> Jesus replied . . . "Your father Abraham rejoiced at the thought of seeing my day; he saw it and was glad."
>
> "You are not yet fifty years old," the Jews said to him, "and you have seen Abraham!"

"I tell you the truth," Jesus answered, "before Abraham was born, I am!" (John 8:56–58 NIV)

Notice two things about that last statement of Jesus: He existed before Abraham; and He identified Himself as God, as the eternal I AM. That is the name we hallow when we pray to the Father in Jesus' name.

What It Means to "Hallow"

A small boy was staying with his grandparents for the summer, and when Sunday rolled around, his grandfather took him to a joyless church service. Just before bed that night, the boy knelt to pray. "Dear God," he said, "thank You that I was able to go to church with my grandpa today . . . but I sure wish You had been there."

In popular modern culture the phrase "Hallowed be Your name" conjures two images. First, a prohibition on swearing. And second, going to a cold church every Sunday morning and singing very dull hymns.

Well, I have news for you. Hallowing God's name is something quite different. Hallowing God's name, in fact, has far more to do with the workweek than it does with Sundays.

Has it occurred to you, for example, why Jesus placed it so near the beginning of the Lord's Prayer? The prayer that God will answer, says Jesus, *first* acknowledges His fatherhood, *then* acknowledges His dominion over the heavens—and then addresses itself to God's name.

This is not the way most people pray. Preoccupied as we are with our own problems, most of us barely have time for a "How d'you do?" before we launch into our grocery list of petitions. We treat God like a telephone shopping service. We are entirely focused on our own needs.

But why this requirement to think first of God's name?

The answer is simple. "Hallowed be Your name" solemnly reminds believers of their responsibility to behave in a way that honors, respects, and brings glory to God. Every day we should seek to enhance God's reputation through the way we live.

You cannot parrot the words "Hallowed be your name" as a pious and well-meaning wish. To say them is to give yourself, heart and soul, to the effort of making them true. You are saying, "Father in heaven, may Your person, Your identity, Your character, Your reputation, Your very being, always be honored." And that will have no cash value unless:

- you know the character of God in Scripture

- you intend to honor and revere that character

- you find that character a source of delight

Naturally, we cannot just pick the things about God that particularly appeal to us and ignore the rest. God's character is a seamless whole. I have heard it described as having six sides, like a cube:

- purity, holiness, flawlessness

- love, compassion, concern

- righteousness, justice, impeccability

- mercy, kindness, longsuffering

- honesty, truth, dependability

- faithfulness, understanding, support

Because each characteristic blends into the rest, any vision of God that sees only a few sides of the "cube" will be distorted and incomplete. Too many people embrace a smorgasbord Christianity. They want to create their own version of God, giving Him only the traits they want to assign Him. They want to choose His love, but not His justice. They want to accept His compassion, but not His purity or righteousness or holiness.

Let me be clear. It does not matter how many heavyweight church leaders or theologians you find to back you up. When you pick and choose, you are not worshiping the God of the Bible. To say "Hallowed be Your name" is to accept God in His entirety. The whole package. No compromise.

We cannot honor and respect—we cannot hallow God's name and bring Him glory—if we do not fully understand and acknowledge His character. As we come to know all His attributes, we can truly praise and glorify Him.

THE KEY TO HALLOWING IS PRAISE

Here is the key to hallowing God's name—the top three attitudes we can cultivate that will magnify and glorify God.

1. Be grateful. We use our hearts and lips to tell God how thankful we are. Do you want to make the devil mad? Express your gratitude to God. How often do we mumble and grumble, complain and sulk? No wonder we give the enemy a foothold in our lives! The secret of victory is sincere gratitude.

2. Be a giver. We give of our substance to God. Not that God needs anything we bring Him, but the discipline of giving makes us more open to His guiding Spirit. Remember, though, that hallowing God's name is not a public relations exercise. What matters is to give, not to give with a fanfare and a press release.

3. Be obedient. We live in obedience to God and His Word. Has it ever occurred to you that when you resist temptation, you glorify the name of God? "I have brought you glory on earth," Jesus prayed to the Father, "by completing the work you gave me to do" (John 17:4 NIV). The same is true for Jesus' disciples. We glorify God by submitting our will to His.

All three of these attitudes—gratitude, giving, and obedience—spring from the same source. They are all aspects of praise and adoration. There is nothing sentimental in this. In its origins, our modern word *adoration* describes the action of kissing the back of the hand—still, in many countries, a customary sign of respect and symbolic submission.

But after a good many years as a minister I have noticed a strange thing. Christians seem to be able to glorify God in one of these ways, or two, but rarely all three at the same time.

Some people have no trouble praising God with gratitude—but ask them to pull out their checkbooks, and you won't see them for the dust in the wake of their hasty retreat. That was probably why the great preacher Clovis Chapel used to say, "I love to preach on giving, because I love to see the generous rejoice and the stingy suffer!"

On the other hand, there are some very generous people who cannot pry their lips apart to thank God in public, and others who find gratitude easy but live lives of shocking compromise and disobedience.

But to pray as Jesus told us, we need all three kinds of praise. When we practice praise, we say to our heavenly Father:

- We recognize Your sovereignty over us.

- We surrender to Your power and authority over us.

- We seek Your dominion over us.

- We gladly place You first in our lives, in every area of our lives.

- We freely submit our wills to Your will.

When all is said and done, you can only have two attitudes in life. Either you put yourself first, or you put God first. And it is only a life filled with praise that allows real prayer to be launched. Such a life decentralizes the self. It puts selfish preoccupations aside to make room for God. That is what Jesus meant when He told us to pray "Hallowed be Your name."

All Christians talk about doing it. Not so many actually walk the talk.

PRAISE WINS THE VICTORY

Without praise, we get too self-conscious. We get preoccupied with who we are, and we forget who God is. We worry too much about what others think of us, and not enough about what God thinks of us.

And then we get grumpy and critical.

Just read what happened to King David when the ark of the covenant was restored to Jerusalem:

> David, wearing a linen ephod, danced before the LORD with all his might, while he and the entire house of Israel brought up the ark of the LORD with shouts and the sound of trumpets.
>
> As the ark of the LORD was entering the City of David, Michal daughter of Saul watched from a window. And when she saw King David leaping and dancing before the LORD, she despised him in her heart . . .
>
> When David returned home to bless his household, Michal daughter of Saul came out to meet him and said, "How the king of Israel has distinguished himself today, disrobing in the sight of the slave girls of his servants as any vulgar fellow would!"
>
> David said to Michal, "It was before the LORD, who chose me rather than your father or anyone from his house when he appointed me ruler over the LORD's people Israel—I will celebrate before the LORD. I will become even more undignified than this, and I will be humiliated in my own eyes. But by these slave girls you spoke of, I will be held in honor."
>
> And Michal daughter of Saul had no children to the day of her death. (2 Sam. 6:14–16, 20–23 NIV)

By coincidence, the Hebrew name *Michal* is the feminine equivalent of my name, Michael, and means the same thing! But Michal seemed unable to muster even a flicker of gratitude for the ark's return. Emotionally she clammed up. Instead of joining in the celebrations, she stood aloof and played the prig. And when her husband came home, all she could do was vent her displeasure. The result? She—and her line—sank into oblivion.

By contrast, the Bible teaches that praise is the secret of victory. It is an essential component of the prayer that God will answer. When people praise, things happen.

Remember how, in the book of Acts, Paul and Silas were arrested in Philippi for preaching the gospel? They were beaten—in our parlance, roughed over with a baseball bat—and left bleeding with their feet in the stocks.

What did Paul and Silas do? Hold an all-night prayer vigil begging God to save them? Not at all. Nor did they complain to God and say "Oh God, we've been faithful in serving you; why are we suffering like this?"

The Bible says they sang and praised God. And in direct response to their praise, an earthquake shook the entire city. The prison gates fell open. And the prison warden was converted to Christ.

That was not an outcome most people would have predicted after witnessing events the day before; then it had seemed more likely Paul and Silas would be tried and stoned. But praise made the difference. It shook off fear—and turned the tables.

Or read the story of King Jehoshaphat in 2 Chronicles 20. This godly king was told, "A vast army is coming against you from Edom, from the other side of the Sea" (v. 2 NIV). In military terms the situation was hopeless. But Jehoshaphat knew the battle was God's. And the next day he took a step that would have most strategists turning in their graves:

> As they set out, Jehoshaphat stood and said, "Listen to me, Judah and people of Jerusalem! Have faith in the LORD your God and you will be upheld; have faith in his prophets and you will be successful." After consulting the people, Jehoshaphat appointed men to sing to the LORD and to praise him for the splendor of his holiness as they went out at the head of the army, saying:

> "Give thanks to the LORD,
>   for his love endures for ever."
>
> (2 Chron. 20:20–21 NIV)

Even as they sang, the enemy coalition collapsed, and by the time Jehoshaphat's forces reached the battlefield, only dead bodies remained. There was so much plunder it took three whole days to collect the spoils of war.

Praise brought the victory.

The Psalms talk about God "inhabiting" the praise of His people. So it's no wonder praise works. Are you a praising person? You should be.

However, a final word of caution is in order.

GOD'S GOOD NAME DEPENDS ON YOU

Do not expect to receive a ringing endorsement from our secular society when you live a lifestyle of praise and gratitude to God. As Paul said, the cross is a stumbling block to the Jews and folly to the Greeks. So do not expect the message of the gospel to be welcomed with open arms. Sometimes it provokes the opposite reaction.

Nevertheless, God wants us to glorify His name through our gratitude, our giving, and our obedience—whether people understand it or not. We should not just accept His good gifts to us—and move on as if nothing had happened. If faith makes no difference to you, how can others believe it will make a difference to them?

Now that you have accepted Christ—now that you're in the family of the heavenly Father—God's reputation rests squarely on you. Every one of us has the power either to credit the name of God or to discredit the name of God. We do one or the other.

Like it or not, we carry the name of Christ. And what we do—or don't do—will reflect directly on Him.

If you have children, you may know what difficulties beset relationships between teenagers and their parents. Teenagers find Mom and

Dad difficult and embarrassing. They don't want to be seen with them. They would rather die than be kissed or hugged in public. And they can act with such insensitivity that parents sometimes despair.

I suspect God's relationship with us sometimes gets into this kind of rut. So much more is possible in a family relationship if children will open up, show a bit of love and appreciation. And with God—whose grasp of good parenting is surely a lot stronger than ours—it only takes a little gratitude, giving, and obedience to put the relationship on an entirely different footing.

The more we are lost in adoration for our God, the more blessed and overwhelmed we will be. If you feel spiritually dry, or you feel that heaven echoes with your prayers like brass, try praise. Develop an "attitude of gratitude." Bless the name of Christ in you—then feel the delight of the Lord!

PRAYER
WORKBOOK

TO REFLECT ON:

As a starting point, think about two difficult circumstances or situations you are facing—situations in which praising God's name is not natural or easy for you. It could be the death or illness of a loved one, a relationship that has soured, a financial need, or a problem on the job. I have written down two difficult situations I have faced. Put your answers in the spaces that follow.

MY ANSWERS

1. When I waited on God to meet a personal need.
2. When my daughter was critically ill in the hospital.

YOUR ANSWERS

1. _____
   _____
2. _____
   _____

As we learn more about the character of God, it becomes easier for us to praise Him while we are enduring the trials of life. Think about the situations or circumstances you described in your previous answer. How can you hallow God's name in this area of your life? How does knowing God's character help you praise Him in this situation? Write down two things you can do to bring glory and honor to God's name through these difficulties.

MY ANSWERS

1. I learned to praise God as Provider—Jehovah Jireh—trusting Him to meet my need.
2. I learned to praise God as Healer—Jehovah Rapha—trusting Him to take care of my daughter.

YOUR ANSWERS

1. _____

   _____
2. _____

   _____

TO READ:

Spend a few minutes quietly reflecting on these Scriptures:

> Your attitude should be the same as that of Christ Jesus:
> Who, being in very nature God,
> > did not consider equality with God something
> > > to be grasped,
> but made himself nothing,
> > taking the very nature of a servant,
> > being made in human likeness.
> And being found in appearance as a man,
> > he humbled himself
> > and became obedient to death—
> > > even death on a cross!
> Therefore God exalted him to the highest place

and gave him the name that is above every name,
   that at the name of Jesus every knee should bow,
     in heaven and on earth and under the earth,
   and every tongue confess that Jesus Christ is Lord,
     to the glory of God the Father.

(Phil. 2:5–11 NIV)

Rejoice in the Lord always. I will say it again: Rejoice! Let your gentleness be evident to all. The Lord is near. Do not be anxious about anything, but in everything, by prayer and petition, with thanksgiving, present your requests to God. And the peace of God, which transcends all understanding, will guard your hearts and your minds in Christ Jesus. (Phil. 4:4–7 NIV)

Shout for joy to the LORD, all the earth.
   Serve the LORD with gladness;
   come before him with joyful songs.
Know that the LORD is God.
   It is he who made us, and we are his;
   we are his people, the sheep of his pasture.
Enter his gates with thanksgiving
   and his courts with praise;
   give thanks to him and praise his name.
For the LORD is good and his love endures forever;
   his faithfulness continues through all generations.

(Psalm 100 NIV)

At once I was in the Spirit, and there before me was a throne in heaven with someone sitting on it. And the one who sat there had the appearance of jasper and carnelian. A rainbow, resembling an emerald, encircled the throne. Surrounding the throne were twenty-four other thrones, and seated on them were twenty-four elders. They were dressed in white and had crowns of gold on their heads . . .

   Whenever the living creatures give glory, honor and thanks to him

who sits on the throne and who lives for ever and ever, the twenty-four
elders fall down before him who sits on the throne, and worship him
who lives for ever and ever. They lay their crowns before the throne
and say:

> "You are worthy, our Lord and God,
>> to receive glory and honor and power,
> for you created all things,
>> and by your will they were created
>> and have their being.

(Rev. 4:2–4, 9–11 NIV)

TO PRAY:

Finally, take a legal pad. Collect all your thoughts and write a prayer
that expresses your adoration for God and exalts His name. As before,
try to avoid using "stock phrases." Make sure that everything you
thank God for, and everything you ask Him for, comes from your heart
and has meaning for you personally. Make the prayer as long or as
short as you wish. When you are satisfied with it, copy it into this
book. Then spend a little time quietly in the presence of your heavenly
Father before speaking it out loud. This is my prayer. Write yours in the
space that follows.

MY PRAYER

Father, because Your name signifies all that You are—Your character,
Your personhood, and Your glory—I want to bless that name. Your
name is my power. Your name is my strength. You have privileged me
by allowing me to take Your name. Just as a wife takes the name of her
husband signifying that she has taken on his identity, I take Your name
today as my identity.

You are the Alpha and the Omega, the beginning and the end. You
are the bishop of my soul and the shepherd of my life. You are my deliv-
erer and my hiding place.

May I today bring honor, not dishonor, to Your name.

May I today bring glory to that precious name.

May I comprehend a little bit of the meaning of the power of Your name.

May the work of my hands and the words of my lips and the thoughts of my mind bring glory to Your name.

May Your name be glorified in the lives of my wife and my children today.

May Your name be glorified in the lives of my staff and the leadership of the church.

May everyone I am associated with today bring glory to Your name.

I adore Your name.

YOUR PRAYER

_____

_____

_____

_____

_____

_____

_____

_____

_____

_____

_____

"YOUR KINGDOM COME"

5

Thrown into Battle

In 1964 I got blackmailed—by my brother Samir.

Math always floored me, and I had been given some really tough homework. Knowing Samir was as bright at math as I was dumb, I decided to risk asking for help. He was working on some scientific experiment of the kind he liked to dabble in.

"You know about algebra, don't you?" I said.

"Need me to do your homework again?"

I felt annoyed that he had seen it coming, but I persevered nevertheless.

"I've got to solve these twenty problems for tomorrow morning."

"How many have you done?"

"Two."

"Show me."

Samir put down the small instrument he was holding and took my schoolbook. After a couple of seconds he shrugged and handed it back to me.

"Sure, I'll help you—"

"Great!" I said, surprised I'd won so easily. "Thanks!"

"—on one condition."

I should have known. "What condition?"

"That you come with me to the evangelistic crusade tonight."

"But why?" I said, calculating how many hours I was going to lose.

"I just want you to come, that's all. Of course, if you want to do your math homework by yourself . . ."

I tried for one last concession. "Okay, but I leave as soon as the sermon's over," I said.

He put his hand out, and we shook on it.

So it was that I ended up hearing a preacher expound on a message from the book of Hosea. It was the passage where God told Hosea to name his daughter Lo-Ruhamah, which literally means "no mercy" in Arabic. God said to Hosea, "I will break the bow of Israel in the Valley of Jezreel . . . For I will no longer have mercy on the house of Israel" (1:5–6 NKJV).

The evangelist talked about how the time for mercy was now, for a judgment day was coming when God would shut the door on us as He had shut it on the house of Israel.

I will no longer have mercy. The message stunned me.

"Okay, you can go home now," my brother said when the sermon had ended and the altar call began.

But I was already on my way to the front to find mercy, to accept Christ. In a space of just twenty-four hours, I had gotten my math homework done—and had my life transformed.

YOU HAVE CHANGED YOUR CITIZENSHIP

What really happens when we come to Christ?

That day in 1964 when I became a Christian parallels another day, twenty years later, when I gained my U.S. citizenship. If you visit my office you will see the certificate on the wall. I put it there because I'm proud of it.

I vividly remember standing in Judge Owen Forrester's courtroom in 1984 and pledging my allegiance to the United States of America. I remember thinking of the millions of immigrants before me who had done the exact same thing, and how precious American freedom is.

People born in America—including my own children—take that freedom for granted. But believe me, when you've lived in a dictatorial state that permits and promulgates religious persecution, you will prize that freedom highly. The certificate of citizenship becomes your guarantee of safety, and your ticket to all the nation's great rights and privileges.

But citizenship also brings responsibilities. In swearing the oath of allegiance, I took it upon myself to live by the laws of the United States. I placed myself not just under the protection but also the authority of the Constitution and the Bill of Rights.

I could not expect to live in America, yet abide by the laws of another country. I could not expect to go through the Constitution with a red pen and cross out all the items that don't suit me. I accepted its duties wholesale. And I accepted the right of my new country to discipline me if I failed to keep the law.

Coming to Christ bears many similarities to taking on a new nationality. On that night back in 1964, I swore an oath of allegiance more rigorous by far than the one I would later swear in an American courtroom—and I do not mean that as a slight on my adopted country. Entry into the kingdom of God is for keeps. It bestows far greater freedoms—and makes far greater demands.

On that day:

- I publicly renounced my allegiance to any other spiritual authority.

- I submitted myself to the kingdom of God and its disciplines.

- I pledged my allegiance to God, who rules the kingdom.

- I accepted His legal authority over me.

- I willingly agreed to obey His Word with all my heart.

- I surrendered all my rights to Him.

You will notice that this amounts to a pretty hefty commitment. I was—in a literal sense—signing my life away. Would I have agreed to surrender all my rights to the U.S. government in Judge Owen Forrester's court-room? I don't think so. Only a totalitarian state would ask such a thing.

So what did I think I was doing by making such a commitment?

Well, the kingdom of God is not a totalitarian state. And here is the difference. Becoming a Christian does indeed involve a complete sub-mission to God. I now accept that:

- His rule over me is supreme.
- I no longer have control over my life.
- I am no longer the captain of my own ship.
- I am no longer the master of my own destiny.

In submitting my old life to God, however, I received a new and far more precious life in return—a life in which I enjoy every freedom and privilege God's kingdom can give. It cost me everything to obtain this spiritual citizenship—but I received *more* than everything back.

And so it is for everyone who comes into the kingdom.

There is another truth that every citizen of the kingdom of God must learn firsthand: *it is a kingdom at war.*

THE BATTLE BEGINS THE DAY YOU JOIN

I don't know where you first received your citizenship for the king-dom. I do know there are preachers out there who give a false impres-sion of what life in the kingdom is like. They say, "If you give your life to Jesus, all your problems will be over. From now on everything will be hunky-dory."

Well, that's not even remotely true. When you join the kingdom of God, you parachute straight into a war zone.

"What?" you say. "Nobody told me that!"

But not so fast! The Bible is explicit about what the Christian life entails. In that sense there are no hidden costs in the gospel. There is no fine print in the contract. Jesus Christ spelled out the terms up front. In the Gospels, for example, we read:

As they were walking along the road, a man said to him, "I will follow you wherever you go."

Jesus replied, "Foxes have holes and birds of the air have nests, but the Son of Man has no place to lay his head." (Luke 9:57–58 NIV)

This is the life of a guerrilla fighter. It is no easy ride. Yes, there is joy, there is companionship, there is unqualified acceptance with God—but you are expected to camp out in the battle zone and fight.

The day I surrendered my life to the Lord Jesus Christ was the day an internal battle in my life began. A firefight broke out inside me. I thank God for the Christian people around me who taught me how to fight and win that war. But many a time I panicked and tried to get myself out of there.

I wanted to take back control, to backtrack on my pledge of allegiance. I found myself trying to renegotiate my initial commitment. In the Middle East we're used to bargaining. Of course, Jesus was a Middle Easterner too—and there's no outbargaining Him!

I would tell God, "I know I said in 1964 that You are my sovereign and king and all that . . . but a few things have come up that I'd like to take care of myself."

You don't need a Ph.D. to know that God does not get excited about renegotiating deals. But usually He gave me a little slack.

In His gracious and infinite wisdom, God would say, "Okay, you want to keep control over this area or that area. Fine. Go for it. Be my guest."

When I first moved to Australia, for example, I tried to postpone my calling to attend seminary and enter the ministry. In spite of God's miraculous provision of a way out of Egypt, I found myself struggling with obedience to His call.

Almost as soon as I arrived, I landed a job with the telephone company. I was able to support myself and move into an apartment while preparing to enroll in seminary. Before the next semester started, however, the telephone company offered me a full scholarship to finish my engineering degree. It sounded like a wonderful opportunity, and I wanted to backtrack on my original plans for coming to Australia.

"I can go into the ministry later," I told myself. "There's no rush. I have the rest of my life to fulfill God's call."

God did not stop me, of course. He let me go right ahead and accept the scholarship.

I'm grateful, however, that my mentor—Donald Robinson, former archbishop of Sydney—helped me realize that I was reneging on my commitment to God. "If He has called you to ministry," he told me, "you should obey that calling now."

With his encouragement, I began to see that I had it backwards. I could always go back later in life and get a university degree (which I did, in fact, although not in engineering), but *now* is always the time to keep your commitment to God.

So I canceled the scholarship and enrolled in seminary. I was learning what citizenship in God's kingdom entails, learning what it means to pray "Your kingdom come."

YOU CAN'T JUST SAY THE WORDS!

In the last chapter I showed how you cannot just pray "Hallowed be Your name," and then stand back to see what happens. You have to reinforce your words with deeds.

It's the same with the kingdom. Every day millions of people around the world say to God, "Your kingdom come." Do they have the slightest comprehension of what they've said? Apparently not. They might as well start their workday by saying "May the next ten hours be productive"—and then go home to bed. It's absurd.

Unpack those three little words—"Your kingdom come"—and you will find what you're really saying is this:

- "King Jesus, rule supreme in my life."

- "King Jesus, dominate my thoughts."
- "King Jesus, reign over every member of my body."
- "King Jesus, exercise full sovereignty over me."
- "King Jesus, let Your program be my preoccupation in life."

Is that what you mean to say? If not, you'd better stop praying!

Please hear me right. The King and His kingdom are inseparable. You cannot take them in isolation. You cannot say that you are a citizen of the kingdom of God without Jesus being the King of your life. If you pray "Your kingdom come," you are saying to the King, "Come and take over."

I know that is a difficult concept to explain to Americans—particularly young people. In America we do not have a supreme ruler, and thank God for that.

But the kingdom of God is not a democracy. God's writ of law runs to its every corner. If you want to live in the kingdom, you must accept the loving and wise rule of the King.

Of course, that affronts our expectations. Left to ourselves, we would want to keep calling the shots and go to God only when we figure we need His help. For most of us, prayer revolves around our own needs, our own plans, our own aspirations.

But such self-obsessed prayer does not get God's attention. It shows that we are behaving like babies—unable to grasp anything beyond our own feelings and wants. The Word of God tells us this is the wrong way to pray!

To pray the prayer that God will answer, you must start from somewhere else. From God's fatherhood, which defines His relationship with us. From His name, which we own and must honor. And from His kingdom, in which we are now citizens and for which we must fight.

That is why Jesus spent so much time telling His disciples about the kingdom. Luke 4:43 says that He came to "preach the good news of the kingdom" (NIV). And for the forty days He remained on earth after the resurrection, He spoke to His disciples "of the things concerning the kingdom of God" (Acts 1:3 NASB).

Teaching the kingdom mattered to Jesus, so it should also matter to us.

If commitment to Jesus Christ brings us citizenship in a kingdom at war—in which we're dropped off behind enemy lines—then who exactly are we fighting? Who is the enemy?

KNOW YOUR ENEMY!

The *other* kingdom is the answer to that question.

For there are two kingdoms in this world. You can belong to one or the other—indeed, you belong to one or the other whether you like it or not—but you cannot belong to both.

On one side is the kingdom of secular power and worldly desire, ultimately ruled over by Satan. On the other is the kingdom of God, which is the domain of God's rule in the hearts and minds of His people.

In spiritual terms there is no such thing as dual citizenship. As Jesus crisply expressed it: "No one can serve two masters. Either he will hate the one and love the other, or he will be devoted to the one and despise the other. You cannot serve both God and Money" (Matt. 6:24 NIV). Ultimately you are driven either by the spirit of evil or by the Holy Spirit of God. Nobody can remain neutral. Nobody will get away with being a double agent.

The outcome of these kingdoms at war is not in doubt. The day will come when all those in God's kingdom will come off the field of battle and live in heaven with God. Satan will be overthrown and cast into the lake of fire, and God's rule will extend unopposed to the limits of the new heaven and new earth.

In the meantime, the world remains under enemy occupation—and we have work to do. We have territory to win.

WHERE IS THE BATTLE HOTTEST?

War is about territory.

Go into the strategy room of an army at war, and you will find a map. This map shows which areas belong to which side. It shows where the main forces of each combatant are concentrated—planes, ships, infantry, tanks, missiles. And between the two sides there runs a line.

That line—it used to be called a "front"—is where the actual fighting takes place. Combat does not go on all the time. In fact, there are periods when everything seems peaceful. But when fighting breaks out, it breaks out somewhere along that line.

If God had a strategy room, He too would have a map, and that map too would have a line. But you would find no continents, roads, rivers, or seas. For the spiritual war between the kingdoms is not fought on land. It is fought in the human will. And the line between the forces goes directly through the middle of every heart on the planet.

For years I did not know this. Right until I went to that crusade meeting with Samir, I had no idea I was living on the battle line. Up to that point the war had been totally quiet. And then I came to Christ. The forces of the Holy Spirit broke out. And the battle began.

It has been going on inside me ever since—just as it does in every Christian—because conversion to Christ is not a *fait accompli*. In all of us there is quite a bit of territory to be won back. The battle rages deep into the personality, liberating piece after piece, bringing every part into conformity with our central and decisive commitment to join the kingdom of God. And at every point and every issue, we find ourselves confronting the same question: Are we going to fight with God, or let Satan hold out?

Sadly, there are Christians who commit to the kingdom and then let themselves be all but overrun by the forces of evil. If only they would put more resources into the fight! Yet even in these cases, the battle will eventually be won, the territory claimed back. For the first, decisive commitment has been made—and once the Holy Spirit has established a bridgehead, there is no going back.

But that threshold must be reached. At the end of the age, on the day of judgment, God will ask you only one question: "To which kingdom do you belong?" What will be your answer? Do you belong to the kingdom of Christ Jesus, or do you belong to the kingdom of this world system?

Don't rely on anything else to save you. Your church membership won't help you. Your denomination won't help you. Your baptism won't help you. Your good works won't help you. Taking communion won't help you. Your political and social connections won't help you.

Only one thing will help you on the day of judgment—and that is showing those spiritual papers that prove you're a citizen of the kingdom of God.

So, when we pray the words "Your kingdom come," we are asking, first, for God to extend His territory in our own lives. We are saying "Lord, take control of every area."

THE BATTLE IN YOU

Of course, the responsibility to let that prayer be answered bounces directly back at us. As Paul wrote to the Corinthians:

> What do righteousness and wickedness have in common? Or what fellowship can light have with darkness? What harmony is there between Christ and Belial? What does a believer have in common with an unbeliever? What agreement is there between the temple of God and idols? For we are the temple of the living God. As God has said: "I will live with them and walk among them, and I will be their God, and they will be my people." . . .
>
> Since we have these promises, dear friends, let us purify ourselves from everything that contaminates body and spirit, perfecting holiness out of reverence for God. (2 Cor. 6:14–16; 7:1 NIV)

What does it take to allow God to extend his territory in our lives? The difference between a defeated Christian and a victorious Christian in this area comes down to one thing: self-discipline. God will only take control of every area of our lives as we yield that control to Him. He will not force us.

Let me illustrate.

I travel overseas quite a bit. Often I will meet someone and say, "Next time you're in Atlanta, come and visit us." And sometimes people take me up on the invitation, for which I am glad.

But imagine my inviting some overseas friend to come and stay in my house—and then not looking after him.

On his arrival I say, "Please feel at home. I want you to have the run of the house. Whatever you want, just help yourself." But before I leave for work, I lock up the refrigerator. I lock up the pantry. I lock up the bathroom. I lock up the dining room. I lock up the living room.

When he wakes up and tries to get into the bathroom, he finds it locked. He goes down to the kitchen to make some breakfast, and he can't open the fridge. Everywhere he goes, the doors are locked. He can't do a thing.

What kind of a host am I? I tell my guest to feel at home—but I confine him to the guest room. Yet many Christians invite Jesus into their lives on exactly that basis. They make a great fanfare of inviting Him in, and then they lock Him up in a single room so He can't change anything around.

Of course we have excuses. "I'm experienced in my job," we say—and we don't let Him into our professional life. "People will never behave any differently," we say—and we don't let Him into our relationships. "I have too many expenses to increase my giving," we say—and we don't let Him into our finances. "I'm well-read and have intelligent opinions," we say—and we don't let Him into our thinking.

And after that, we get down on our knees and pray "Your kingdom come."

What in the world do we think we're doing? We simply cannot ask God to come into our lives, and then tell Him that most of it is off-limits. That is as pointless as going into battle on your own, armed with a stick.

But we are asking a second thing when we pray "Your kingdom come." And that is for God's kingdom to advance elsewhere on the battle line—in the lives of others.

THE BATTLE FOR OTHERS

Parents who pray "Your kingdom come" are praying on behalf of their children: "Lord, may You rule and dominate the lives of our children. May Your authority be established in their hearts. May Your Word be hidden in them, and may Your Kingdom be preeminent in their lives."

Church leaders who pray "Your kingdom come" are praying for those they serve through leadership: "Lord, may Your program—and not ours—be established in our church. May Your Word—and not our opinions—be the ultimate authority. May Your will be established in our decision-making and planning, and may You be the supreme ruler and the ultimate authority in our church."

And, of course, we absolutely must pray for those still outside the kingdom. "Lord, may those under Satan's rule turn to You and seek liberation. May those who are citizens of the kingdom of Satan become citizens of Your Kingdom. May those who mistakenly think they are Christians, simply because they go to church, be delivered from their delusion and come under Your authority. Lord, may You increase the number of citizens of the kingdom of heaven on this earth."

As citizens of the kingdom of heaven, we are headed for an eternal city, where we will dwell forever with God.

THE BUS TO HEAVEN

Yet many Christians are like the little boy who heard a sermon on heaven. The preacher brought his message to a dramatic climax by calling out to the congregation, "All of you who are ready for heaven, stand up."

Everybody stood except for this young boy.

The preacher looked puzzled and said, "Son, don't you want to go to heaven?"

"Oh yes . . . I do!" the boy replied.

"Then why didn't you stand up?" the preacher asked.

"I thought you were taking a bus load right now."

Like the lad in this story, many of us have a tendency to drag our feet when it comes to making progress toward heaven. We are often lax, often want to leave the fighting to someone else.

Yet the psalmist said, "I would rather be a doorkeeper in the house of my God than dwell in the tents of the wicked" (Ps. 84:10 NIV). And Paul told the Corinthian church that our bodies are the "temple of the Holy Spirit" (1 Cor. 6:19 NIV), who is in us.

Each of us, then, is the gatekeeper at the door of his or her own soul. Our job is to ensure that the doors of the temple are closed to defilements—closed, that is, to anything that could damage the interior. Every faculty is a door. Each of us has an eye gate, an ear gate, a mind gate. And one of our responsibilities is to ensure that nothing gets through those gates that shouldn't be there. It requires vigilance on our part.

There is no use praying, "Your kingdom come" unless you intend to remain alert. The kingdom of God is not a geographical domain. It is an inner condition of mind and spirit, in which God's will should progressively become our own.

So think carefully about what citizenship means in the kingdom of God.

You may not yet have taken the oath of allegiance to God's kingdom, and therefore you're still on the wrong side. If so, don't be fooled into thinking that everybody goes to heaven "as long as they're good." It's citizenship that counts. You need to make a choice.

You may be trying to keep a foot in both camps, up to your neck in this world system, but going to church "just in case." If so, you're mistaken. That is not the way God works. You need to make a choice.

Or you may be a citizen of the kingdom of God, but one who has been locking God out of many areas of your life. Many Christians are like that. But let me tell you very simply: either He is the Lord of all, or He is not Lord at all. You need to make a choice.

One day the battle will be over. The "bus to heaven" will really leave. So if you don't long for heaven, if you don't long for the complete rule of God, if you don't long to be with Jesus—then think again about praying "Your kingdom come." Because that is exactly what you're asking God to do.

PRAYER WORKBOOK

TO REFLECT ON:

As a starting point, think about a time when you arrived in a new situation and took on new responsibilities. Changing jobs, for example, or going to a new school. What would you say were the two main challenges you faced in making a success of that new venture? I have written down two things I found challenging about new situations. Put your answers in the spaces that follow.

MY ANSWERS

1. When I was eleven years old, I changed schools without telling my father. It was a better school with better teachers, and as a result I did better academically.
2. In 1969 I left Egypt and lived in Lebanon for some time. I knew no one at first but made many friends within a short period of time.

YOUR ANSWERS

1. _____

   _____

2. _____

   _____

No change we experience can match the move we make from the kingdom of the world to the kingdom of heaven. But sometimes we draw on the same strengths. Think again about the new situation you named above, and ask yourself what qualities the challenge brought out in you—perhaps qualities you did not know you had. Write these down in the spaces below, and say whether you think these God-given qualities play a part in your discipleship.

MY ANSWERS

1. I discovered that I am an initiator and a risk taker, and this is an ability that God has developed in me over the years. It helped me fulfill His call to start a new church.
2. Arriving as a stranger in a new country, I got to the end of my own resources very quickly; at that point I learned what it meant to totally depend on God.

YOUR ANSWERS

1. _____
   _____
2. _____
   _____

TO READ:

Spend a few minutes quietly reflecting on these Scriptures:

As for you, you were dead in your transgressions and sins, in which you used to live when you followed the ways of this world and of the ruler of the kingdom of the air, the spirit who is now at work in those who are disobedient. All of us also lived among them at one time, gratifying the cravings of our sinful nature and following its desires and thoughts. Like the rest, we were by nature objects of wrath. But because of his great love for us, God, who is rich in mercy, made us alive with Christ even when we were dead in transgressions—it is by grace you have been saved. And God raised us up with Christ and seated us with him in the heavenly realms in Christ Jesus, in order that in the coming ages he might show the incomparable riches of his grace, expressed in his kindness to us in Christ Jesus. (Eph. 2:1–7 NIV)

Submit yourselves, then, to God. Resist the devil and he will flee from you. Come near to God and he will come near to you. Wash your hands, you sinners, and purify your hearts, you double-minded. Grieve, mourn and wail. Change your laughter to mourning and your joy to gloom. Humble yourselves before the Lord, and he will lift you up. (James 4:7–10 NIV)

Once again, the kingdom of heaven is like a net that was let down into the lake and caught all kinds of fish. When it was full, the fishermen pulled it up on the shore. Then they sat down and collected the good fish in baskets, but threw the bad away. This is how it will be at the end of the age. (Matt. 13:47–48 NIV)

TO PRAY:

Finally, take a legal pad. Collect all your thoughts and write a prayer that expresses how the kingdom of God affects your life. As before, try to avoid using "stock phrases." Make sure that everything you thank God for, and everything you ask Him for, comes from your heart and has meaning for you personally. Make the prayer as long or as short as you wish. When you are satisfied with it, copy it into this book. Then spend a little time quietly in the presence of your heavenly Father before speaking it out loud. This is my prayer. Write yours in the space that follows.

MY PRAYER

Father, first and foremost, I seek Your kingdom to come in every area of my life.

May there be no facet of my life where Your rule is not supreme. Reign supreme, oh my King. Be enthroned in my heart today.

May there be no rivals for You.

May no other thought preoccupy me.

May all actions I perform be inspired by Your Spirit.

Let Your rule and kingdom come to my wife and my children today. May they continue to know the joy of allowing Your rule to take hold over their lives.

Let Your kingdom rule supreme in my ministry, so that Your perfect will, and not my own wisdom, underlies the work You have given me to do.

Finally, I long for Your supreme rule to extend from heaven to earth.

Oh, how I long for Your return, Lord Jesus!

On that day, our imperfection will be made perfect, and the rule of worldly governments will give way to Your wise and just dominion. Come soon, Lord Jesus!

YOUR PRAYER

_____

_____

_____

_____

_____

_____

_____

_____

_____

"Your Will Be Done"

6

Discerning God's Will

A Christian with a serious obesity problem once decided he would go on a diet and lose some weight. He was addicted to gooey cakes, and a major part of his weight-loss strategy involved changing his route to work so he would not drive past the pastry shop.

The first week went well. He drove to work a different way, and never went in the bakery once. He lost six pounds.

But in the middle of the second week, his plan was shot to pieces. His colleagues watched in amazement as he shuffled into the office carrying the most fattening piece of pastry they had ever seen.

"We thought you were on a diet!" they said.

"It's God's will for me to eat this cake," he replied.

How, they wanted to know, did he reach this conclusion?

"Simple," he said. "You see, by mistake this morning I took my old route to work, the one that goes past the pastry shop. And when I saw what I had done, I began to pray. 'Lord,' I said, 'just today should I go in and get a pastry? After all, I didn't come this way on purpose. And I've been doing very well for over a week.'

"And God told me, 'If you find a parking space in front of the bakery, you can go and eat the pastry.' And you know what? I went around the block six times, and lo and behold, the seventh time there was a parking spot right in front!"

We can all laugh at a story like that. The reluctant dieter was obviously trying to rationalize his out-of-control sweet tooth as being God's will.

Yet all of us struggle at times with the problem of discerning God's will.

TWO PROBLEMS WITH THE WILL OF GOD

Actually, Christians have two problems with the will of God.

The first one—which is quite sincere and understandable—is how to figure out what God's will is.

It is one of the most frequently asked questions in the church: "How do I know the will of God?" Believers ask it from one side of the planet to the other. A big decision comes up, and they want to be sure they're jumping the right way. Should I marry this person or not? Should I take this job or not? Should I make this move or not? Should I get involved in this ministry or not?

Almost always the issue is specific to the person concerned and has no obvious answer in the Word of God. You can read the Bible from cover to cover, and you won't find any advice on whether you should marry Barney or Chuck. Nor will it tell you whether joining Microsoft is a shrewd career move, or whether Pittsburgh is a better place to raise your kids than Detroit. The Bible remains neutral on such things.

But there is a second problem with the will of God, which is the one that dogged the obese man mentioned above. And this problem is that sometimes we know jolly well what God wants us to do—*and we don't want to do it.*

Did you identify with the mind games that man played over his gooey cake? Of course you did. It's human nature. We want to do a wrong thing, and we know we only have three options:

- Forget about it and do the right thing instead.

- Do the wrong thing and be shameless about it.

- Find a way of proving that the wrong thing is really right.

We don't want to do the first. We can't bring ourselves to do the second. So the third is all we have left. We want to indulge ourselves, and at the same time hold on to at least a bit of our integrity. The excuses we come up with are pretty old hat. "Just this once." Or, "God knows I'm only human; He won't mind."

Have you said something like that to yourself recently? If so, you have a problem with the will of God.

And it is *His* will—not yours—that is the crux of the matter.

ARE YOU A SPIRITUAL BEGGAR?

You have figured out by now that you cannot glibly ask God to do things—and then refuse to be in on the action. "Hallowed be Your name" makes demands on us. So does "Your kingdom come." And so does "Your will be done on earth as it is in heaven." When you pray that, you're asking for radical change.

But, of course, this runs contrary to the whole mind-set of our culture.

Our society is now dominated by need. Our focus lies entirely on what other people—including the government—should be doing for us. Television advertising bombards us, day in and day out, telling us what our needs are so we can go to the stores and have our needs met. Slick politicians run around telling us what our needs are so we can vote for them and have our needs met. As a society, we are one seething mass of unfulfilled need.

The same thinking has overrun every part of life.

Husbands and wives look at each other and ask, "How are you going to meet my needs?" Employers and employees look to each other and ask, "How are you going to meet my needs?" The same cancer has even crept into the church. Why else do we do all this serving and ministering to one another? Why else do people wander from church to church looking for a congregation that makes them feel good?

Encouraged to inflate our expectations, we come to God with a mindset that says, "Give me happiness, give me wealth, give me opportunity, give me help." What *we* want always comes first. We have turned ourselves into a church of spiritual beggars.

But this is not the pattern of prayer left to us by Jesus.

Praying "You," Not "I"

Look at the wording of the prayer Jesus taught his disciples: "Hallowed be *Your* name. *Your* Kingdom come. *Your* will be done."

Where is the emphasis placed?

Not on the person praying, but on the Person prayed to. Of course, you might think this is a kind of self-abandonment, with no guarantees that God will keep His side of the bargain. But remember that Almighty God is not a remote figure. The Person who created and controls the universe also came down to be born a human being, among the poorest of the poor.

God knows what it is to need. The One who caused water to burst from the rocks for the Israelites had to ask a woman to bring Him a simple drink from a well. The One robed in splendor in the courts of heaven was stripped naked and nailed to a cross. The One who created the galaxies had to build fires to shield Himself from the winter cold.

Meeting human need, then, is very much on God's agenda. Human needs are not irrelevant or unspiritual. I am not saying that human beings should be valued only in spiritual and non-material terms. Poverty is real and degrading. Disease and hunger are tragedies crying out for a solution.

But the fact remains: when Jesus taught us how to pray, He did not instruct us to fall on our knees and say, "O Lord, solve my problems!" He said:

This is how you should pray:
"Our Father in heaven,
hallowed be your name,
your kingdom come,
your will be done
on earth as it is in heaven." (Matt. 6:9–10 NIV)

Why? Because Jesus knew that when needs become our focus, they soon become our god. And then we are in a worse state than before. "Your will be done" not only puts the horse where it belongs—before the cart—it also establishes the only grounds on which our pressing needs can be met.

WHY GOD'S WILL IS GOOD FOR US

But at this point most of us ask a question.

After all, doing the will of God does not—on the face of it—sound very interesting or exciting. The phrase has the same kind of feel about it as "doing what you're told" or "sticking to the rules." What, then, is the real advantage of doing things God's way?

Let me illustrate it for you.

A ship was transporting a number of rare South American birds back to French Guiana for release into the wild. In the middle of the voyage, and several hundred miles from the nearest land, one of the birds got out of its cage. Efforts to recapture it in the hold failed dismally, and in the end the bird made it onto the deck and escaped from the ship altogether.

At that point nothing more could be done. The sailors watched helplessly as it flew up into the sky, and then, giving it up for lost, went back to their normal duties.

But the next day the same bird reappeared. It collapsed on the deck, bedraggled and exhausted, and showed no resistance as one of the crew picked it up and returned it to its cage. Flying non-stop above the ocean, it had found nowhere to rest, and consequently returned to the ship.

Now, I do not want to suggest that the Christian life resembles being transported in a cage! But the ship at sea provides a good analogy for God's will. Flying off into the blue may feel like liberation, but it is short-lived. In the end, the ocean provides no resting place. The only place of safety from the winds and storms is the ship.

Those who know the Lord Jesus Christ and walk with Him daily will know just how fulfilling a life of obedience is—whatever it may look like from the outside. The only true joy in life is to know that you are bending your will to God's. Paradoxically, freedom lies where you might least expect it: in submission to God's authority and God's Word. Flying off on your own may seem to meet your needs. But in the end it does the opposite.

Like the bird, we are built to live in the place the "ship" is taking us. Life on the ocean waves may not suit us all the time, but it is the one sure way to get where we really need to go. Just as the bird was finally released into the rain forests, so we will find our true place and ultimate fulfillment in heaven. It is because we trust God to get us there safely that we pray, "Your will be done on earth as it is in heaven."

Doing God's will—all the time, with conscious commitment and effort—is serious business. No wonder Jesus said, "Not everyone who says to me, 'Lord, Lord,' will enter into the kingdom of heaven, but only he who does the will of my Father who is in heaven" (Matt. 7:21 NIV).

People can claim to be Christians until they are blue in the face. But if they are not living in obedience to the will of God, we may doubt whether they ever seriously made a first commitment—whether, in the terms of the last chapter, they bothered to sign their citizenship papers.

How to Obey God—and Enjoy It!

I confess that there are areas of my own life where I find doing the will of God a struggle. One area where I have difficulty is in receiving graciously from other people. Over twenty years ago God showed me I had a problem with that.

Perhaps it stems from pride or self-sufficiency—I don't know. But it comes very hard to me. I'm a minister, and I'm used to being the one who ministers to others; consequently, it is sometimes hard for me to receive ministry from someone else—even when it's a direct answer to prayer.

I may have been praying earnestly for God's provision for a certain need—and then I balk when He sends that provision through a person rather than simply dropping it out of heaven like manna. But God most often works through people; it's just the way He operates. And my job is not to second-guess Him, but to thank Him and receive the answer—even if it makes me feel uncomfortable for a while.

I used to pray hard over this problem about receiving graciously from other people, saying, "Okay, Lord, now You take care of this and fix it."

He hasn't fixed it—hasn't fixed me—yet, and I still struggle. Some people would advise me, "Hey, that's just the way you are. Don't give yourself grief over it. Accept yourself."

But I know the issue is important. God wants me to be at the very center of His will. And it is no good excusing myself on the grounds that my shortcomings are just the way God made me. It's not true. In the power of the Holy Spirit I *can* do whatever He asks of me. And while I am dogged by imperfection and original sin like everyone else in this world, that does not make my errors God's fault. God is not the author of evil.

And here's a secret.

Some Christians focus entirely on the places in their lives where they find doing God's will difficult. And consequently they are forever gritting their teeth. Sometimes they grit their teeth so hard you think their jaws will explode. But obedience to God has many facets. And the best way to increase it is to keep your main attention directed to areas where you *do* obey and *do* get things right.

Why not enjoy the journey of obedience? Why not have fun, melding your will with the will of God? For the Bible often associates obedience with joy and refreshment. The psalmist said, "I delight to do Your will, O my God" (Ps. 40:8 NKJV). Jesus said, "If you keep my commandments, you will abide in My love," and "You are My friends if you do whatever I command you" (John 15:10, 14 NKJV).

Doing the will of God brings satisfaction and joy. Christians who go around sulking, with long faces, are an embarrassment to God. Who would want that kind of Christianity? It is one of the great missions of Christian faith today to rediscover the sheer joy and pleasure and contentment of doing what God wants. Because that's what faith should be like. Like heaven.

There are no miseries in heaven. There is no hardship or pain in heaven. Only contentment, and joy, and perfect peace. When you enjoy doing the will of God, you are bringing heaven into your heart. Do you want a piece of heaven on earth? Obey the will of God.

HOW TO FIGURE OUT THE WILL OF GOD

Finally, I want to come back to the problem I mentioned at the beginning of this chapter. How can we know what the will of God is in any given situation?

It is one thing to live in obedience to God when confronted with clear, moral choices. It is another thing when both options seem equally worthy and have equal potential. Job A versus Job B. Church C versus Church D. Home E versus Home F. And so on. How on earth do we determine what God wants us to do?

Let me take you back to a scriptural precedent—the Council at Jerusalem, recorded in Acts 15, where the leaders of the mainly Jewish early church had to rule on the contentious issue of whether Gentile Christians should be circumcised and keep the law of Moses:

> The apostles and elders met to consider this question. After much discussion, Peter got up and addressed them: "Brothers, you know that

some time ago God made a choice among you that the Gentiles might hear from my lips the message of the gospel and believe. God, who knows the heart, showed that he accepted them by giving the Holy Spirit to them, just as he did to us. He made no distinction between us and them, for he purified their hearts by faith. Now then, why do you try to test God by putting on the necks of the disciples a yoke that neither we nor our fathers have been able to bear? No! We believe it is through the grace of our Lord Jesus that we are saved, just as they are."

The whole assembly became silent as they listened to Barnabas and Paul telling about the miraculous signs and wonders God had done among the Gentiles through them. When they finished, James spoke up: "Brothers, listen to me. Simon has described to us how God at first showed his concern by taking from the Gentiles a people for himself. The words of the prophets are in agreement with this, as it is written:

> "'After this I will return
> and rebuild David's fallen tent.
> Its ruins I will rebuild,
> and I will restore it.
> that the remnant of men may seek the Lord,
> and all the Gentiles who bear my name,'
> says the Lord, who does these things
> that have been known for ages.

"It is my judgment, therefore, that we should not make it difficult for the Gentiles who are turning to God." (Acts 15:16–19 NIV)

This Scripture passage contains most of the points in my personal program for discerning God's will. These are the things I try to do:

1. **Check the Word of God.** First I ask myself whether my proposed course of action is consistent with Scripture. This is exactly what James did at the Council. He measured the idea of the gospel for Gentiles

against the yardstick of biblical prophecy and found that they dove-tailed together perfectly. So look first at the Word of God. If you do not feel confident enough to do it yourself, ask a godly Christian to help you. Do you find a contradiction? Then drop your plan immediately. If not, go on to the next step.

2. **Check your experience.** Once again, this happened in the story recounted in Acts. Peter recalled that God had already spoken to him on a very similar issue. In other words, a precedent had already been laid down. So ask yourself: "Have I faced this situation or a situation like this before? What did God show me then?" God is consistent. If you got it wrong last time, learn from your mistake.

3. **Seek advice.** Especially if the decision is crucial, or a close call, get prayerful counsel. Other people will often have a breadth of perspective that you do not have. Don't ask them to make up your mind for you, but take their views seriously and weigh them carefully. That was why the early church came together to discuss the Gentile issue. Peter and James were two of the wisest men around. God had spoken to them before. Their advice was worth seeking.

4. **Don't fudge the issue.** The believers at the Council who wanted everyone—Gentiles included—to observe the law of Moses, apparently honored the Council's decision. Do the same. Sometimes an idea seems so exciting or so compelling that we are tempted to stay with it no matter what. That is nearly always a mistake. God is smarter than even the wisest of men. Don't get carried away.

5. **Be patient.** It is a weakness of our generation to want everything decided immediately. But there is no equivalent of the "one-minute manager" in the Christian church. Delay does not mean denial. Rather, it lends useful perspective, and enables you to see your options with a little more objectivity. No doubt it took many months to convene the Council in Jerusalem, but the consensus reached at that meeting was vital to the health of the church; the question did not call for a hasty decision.

6. **If confused, admit it.** Sometimes I say to the Lord, "I am dumb. I am not intelligent enough to make a choice. Just close all the doors except the one that I am supposed to go through." That is not a cop-out. Sometimes situations are too complex for us to come to a right decision. The Bible says that God protects the simple. If you need Him to make things absolutely clear, then ask.

And one more thing.

Some people are so hung up on doing the will of God, they won't get out of bed in the morning unless God gives them a word. They go to God with every pesky little decision they have to make, and expect Him to point them in the right direction. This is nonsense. If God had meant you to ask for confirmation over which breakfast cereal to eat, He would not have bothered giving you decision-making ability.

What shines through above all else about the Council in Jerusalem is that everyone present argued the matter through. They used their God-given capacity to reason. Then they came to a solution that made sense.

As it happens, some did not think it was quite the *right* decision. What James proposed—and what the Council agreed to—was that Gentiles should be asked to observe the Ten Commandments, in addition to a commitment not to eat the meat of strangulated animals.

Did it matter?

Probably not. We do not always get our decisions exactly right. But we can get them "right enough" if we handle our decision making prayerfully. So pray "Your will be done on earth as it is in heaven," and then try your best to live as God would want you to.

You will never make right decisions in a life of disobedience. Or when you're angry and resentful at God. Or when you're being flagrantly disobedient to Scripture. But as you submit to the Word of God, you will ultimately do the will of God.

PRAYER WORKBOOK

TO REFLECT ON:

As a starting point, think about two really good decisions you have made in the past. By "good" I mean that you now look back on them with satisfaction and feel that you made the right choice before God. I have recorded a couple of decisions I feel good about. Put your answers in the spaces that follow.

MY ANSWERS

1. In 1987 I planted a new church in Atlanta, even though many people thought it was a bad idea, and I was supported by only one or two godly, praying friends.
2. In 1977 I moved to the United States, even though many of my friends and family wanted me to stay in Australia. But God clearly was leading me.

YOUR ANSWERS

1. _____

_____

2. _____

_____

We make choices for many different reasons and with many different consequences. For the two decisions you recorded above, say what makes you certain now that you chose in accordance with God's will. It may be that you are more convinced of this now than you were at the time. Put your answers beneath mine in the spaces provided.

MY ANSWERS

1. God has blessed thousands of lives through this decision to plant a church.
2. I experienced the peace of God in making a decision not everyone approved.

YOUR ANSWERS

1. _____

_____

2. _____

_____

TO READ:

Spend a few minutes quietly reflecting on these Scriptures:

> Teach me, O LORD, to follow your decrees;
> then I will keep them to the end.
> Give me understanding, and I will keep your law
> and obey it with all my heart.
> Direct me in the path of your commands,
> for there I find delight.
> Turn my heart toward your statutes
> and not towards selfish gain.
> Turn my eyes away from worthless things;
> renew my life according to your word.
> (Ps. 119:33–37 NIV)

For it is God's will that by doing good you should silence the ignorant talk of foolish men. Live as free men, but do not use your freedom as a cover-up for evil; live as servants of God. Show proper respect to everyone: Love the brotherhood of believers, fear God, honor the king. (1 Peter 2:15–17 NIV)

Then Jesus went with his disciples to a place called Gethsemane, and he said to them, "Sit here while I go over there and pray." He took Peter and the two sons of Zebedee along with him, and he began to be sorrowful and troubled. Then he said to them, "My soul is overwhelmed with sorrow to the point of death. Stay here and keep watch with me."

Going a little farther, he fell with his face to the ground and prayed, "My Father, if it is possible, may this cup be taken from me. Yet not as I will, but as you will." (Matt. 26:36–39 NIV)

TO PRAY:

Finally, take a legal pad. Collect all your thoughts and write a prayer in which you try to come to terms with the will of God for your life. As before, try to avoid using "stock phrases." Make sure that everything you thank God for, and everything you ask Him for, comes from your heart and has meaning for you personally. Make the prayer as long or as short as you wish. When you are satisfied with it, copy it into this book. Then spend a little time quietly in the presence of your heavenly Father before speaking it out loud. This is my prayer. Write yours in the space that follows.

MY PRAYER

Father, it is clear that Your perfect will is not perfectly executed on the earth as it is executed in heaven. I look around and I see wickedness and evil, violence, disease, and death. Even among Your people there is more intensity about accomplishing our wills than seeking Yours.

Help me today not to fall into the trap of trying to answer my own prayers, or seeking to accomplish my own program. Do not leave me to my own ambitions.

Today I seek Your perfect will in my life and in my family's life.

I long for Your perfect will to be accomplished in my work and among all those with whom I will come into contact.

In the times when I am not able to discern Your will, give me the patience to wait. Help me today not to jump ahead of You or to lag behind You. And, Father, once I discover Your will, give me the courage to joyfully embrace it and willingly obey it.

Father, just as Your will is perfectly executed in heaven, let it be executed on earth. And especially may Your will be done in Your church, and in the lives of all those who confess the name of Your son, Jesus.

YOUR PRAYER

"OUR DAILY BREAD"

7

God Looks After His Own

Dr. Jerome Frank, professor of psychiatry at Johns Hopkins University, knows a lot about the fear of flying. He knows a lot because every time he gets on a plane and his fellow passengers find out he's a psychiatrist, they tell him how scared they are.

Way back in the days before metal detectors and security checks, a passenger in the next seat confided to him, "I used to be deathly anxious about flying. It all started when a man brought a bomb on board a flight to Denver to kill his mother-in-law. I became worried sick every time I flew after that incident. I always wondered which passenger was carrying a bomb."

"What did you do about it?" Dr. Frank asked him.

"I went to one of those special classes for people afraid to fly, and they told me that there's only one chance in 100,000 that I would be on the same flight as someone with a bomb."

"Did that make you feel better?"

"Are you kidding?" the passenger said. "At one in 100,000 you're almost certain to get blown up sooner or later. But this is what I figured out," he went on. "I reasoned that if the chances of one bomb being on a plane were one in 100,000, the chances of *two bombs* being on the plane would be into the billions. Those odds I knew I could live with."

Dr. Frank became intrigued. "But what good would that do you?"

"Plenty," said the man. And at that point he lifted his attaché case carefully onto his lap and whispered, "You see, ever since then I've carried a bomb in my hand luggage."

YOU EITHER TRUST OR WORRY

I suspect Dr. Frank gilded this tale in retelling it!

Nevertheless, it illustrates an important point: once worry gets a foothold, it very easily invades your whole thought process.

This happens in spite of the fact that most worries have only the slimmest foundation in fact. Studies show, in fact, that the average person is anxious about future things that will never happen, or things in the past that can't be changed.

I learned an interesting fact recently. A dense fog—extensive enough to cover seven city blocks to a depth of a hundred feet—is composed of *less than one glass of water*. Atomized into sixty thousand million droplets, one glass of water can throw a whole city center into confusion. A few gallons could cripple an entire metropolitan area.

Worry works exactly like that. One small worry fogs up your whole consciousness. It creeps into every corner, distracting your attention, making you underperform, spoiling your enjoyment of life. A small glass of worry goes a long, long way.

The English term *worry* comes from the old German word meaning to "strangle" or "choke." Which is pretty much the long-term effect of worrying. Like a rocking chair, it keeps you moving without getting you anywhere. Left to itself, like a small stream, it finally cuts a channel so wide that your whole flow of concentration gets diverted. The longer it goes on, the harder it is to shift.

Not surprisingly, worry is a widespread problem, and most books about it treat worrying as a medical disorder. In some severe cases this may be true. Worry can have deep-rooted causes and pass beyond a person's control. But ordinary, garden-variety worry of the kind we all experience is not a disorder. It is a sin.

Am I being too hard on worriers? After all, mention the word *sin* and most people start thinking of the big ones—murder, adultery, and theft. Not many Christians would dare to name worry as a sin. But let's call a spade a spade. Worry directly contradicts the command to trust in God. Worry is trust in the negative. It spurns God's promises of provision to the faithful believer and makes him act as though God did not exist.

In my book, that's a sin. The issue is not psychological but theological. Christians should not worry. They should pray, as Jesus instructed, "Give us this day our daily bread."

GOD PROVIDES FOR THOSE WHO OBEY HIM

Let's look first at the word *bread* in this portion of the Lord's Prayer. In the West we have so much bread we end up throwing it in the garbage. We do not ask God to give us bread—all we have to do is go to the grocery store and buy it. More than that, like the man with the gooey cakes, our problem with bread is not in getting too little but in eating too much of it. It could be argued, then, that this line of the Lord's Prayer has no relevance to Westerners; only people in poorer places need to pray it.

But, of course, "daily bread" here stands for much more than food. We are praying for God to give us what we need—and that means not just food, but warmth, shelter, income, companionship, and everything else up to peace and personal fulfillment.

In the last chapter, though, you will remember that obsession with need is not the starting point for prayer. In the model Jesus left us, prayer forces us to deal with things *we should be doing for God* long before we get to things that *God should be doing for us*. As we have seen, three powerful priorities stand out:

- the name of God—*Hallowed be Your name*

- the kingdom of God—*Your kingdom come*

- the will of God—*Your will be done*

Does this mean God does not care about our needs? Not at all. Right at the heart of God's purpose for us is that we should enjoy His blessing in material, psychological, and spiritual ways.

But there is a sense of order here. God is there for us—if we are living for Him. When your life's focus is God, then God's focus is your needs. When your life's focus is the glory of God, then God's focus is your provision. When your life's focus is to bring honor to His name, then His focus is every detail of your life. Do you want God to live for you? Then you must live for Him. That, as they say, is the deal.

The prayer that God will answer is the prayer that springs from a life of commitment and obedience. Telling you that is not a cop-out. Some preachers will promise you God's health and wealth, then when you don't receive those things, they will load you up with guilt for letting God down. That is not what I am saying. I am simply telling you that Jesus linked obedience and blessing together. You don't have to be a hermit. But your priorities have to be right.

Paul the apostle understood this connection only too well.

PLENTY TO WORRY ABOUT

The letter Paul wrote to the Philippian church was among his last. And since he was in prison at the time, you would expect him to have every reason for feeling glum. But even the prospect of his approaching death did not seem to faze him. "Even if I am being poured out like a drink offering on the sacrifice and service coming from your faith," he wrote, "I am glad and rejoice with all of you. So you too should be glad and rejoice with me" (Phil. 2:17–18 NIV).

Yes, Paul had plenty to worry about. And yet he did not worry. On the contrary, he rejoiced. To see how he had his priorities in order, read this section from the end of the letter:

Do not be anxious about anything, but in everything, by prayer and petition, with thanksgiving, present your requests to God. And the peace of God, which transcends all understanding, will guard your hearts and your minds in Christ Jesus . . .

I rejoice greatly . . . that at last you have renewed your concern for me. Indeed, you have been concerned, but you had no opportunity to show it. I am not saying this because I am in need, for I have learned to be content whatever the circumstances. I know what it is to be in need, and I know what it is to have plenty. I have learned the secret of being content in any and every situation, whether well fed or hungry, whether living in plenty or in want. I can do everything through him who gives me strength.

Yet it was good of you to share in my troubles . . . for even when I was in Thessalonica, you sent me aid again and again when I was in need. Not that I am looking for a gift, but I am looking for what may be credited to your account. I have received full payment and even more; I am amply supplied, now that I have received from Epaphroditus the gifts you sent. They are a fragrant offering, an acceptable sacrifice, pleasing to God. And my God will meet all your needs according to his glorious riches in Christ Jesus. (Phil. 4:6–7, 10–14, 16–19 NIV)

There are three things worth noting in this passage.

First, Paul was quite candid about being in need. He was not afraid to speak frankly of his hardships—though clearly he did not do so as a way of "fishing" for other people's help.

Second, his life of faith had taught him to put his needs firmly in the back seat. He had worked virtually unsupported in foreign countries, and now he had been thrown into prison. Both situations would have most of us feeling pretty sorry for ourselves. But in his passion to see God's will done, Paul had learned to take everything else as it came.

Third, God met Paul's needs through other Christians. We can infer from the Scripture passage quoted above that the Philippian church had been providing for Paul over many years. And, Paul said, they were not going to miss their reward. In God's economy, meeting the needs of others is a sure way to have your own needs met. Prayer and action go hand in hand.

Do you want to overcome worry and anxiety? Then understand God's order of priority. Needs are real and can be pressing. But difficulties should never consume you. Choose to trust, and the worries will be taken care of.

Well, that's all very easy to say. And you could object—with some justification—that a comfortable middle-aged minister in a wealthy Atlanta church has no right to lecture people on trusting God for necessities.

IT REALLY WORKS!

If that's what you're thinking, let me assure you that I've "been there and done that."

In the winter of 1977–78 we were living in California. I was attending graduate school. My wife, Elizabeth, was at home with two children—two preschool children—and a third on the way. We had to live on less than seventy-five hundred dollars a year—which was little enough even in the seventies. Yet we still sought to be faithful with our tithe.

One day I got my statement from the bank.

"We've got fifty dollars," I told my wife.

"It's enough for groceries," she replied.

"It's our tithe," I said.

We looked at each other. In obedience to my commitment, I wrote out a check for fifty dollars and sent it in the mail, hoping that it would take a long time to clear—long enough for something else to turn up.

When I say we had nothing else, I mean we had nothing at all. Not even anything to sell. As I have already confessed, I am not a person who is given to asking others for help, even if my life depends on it.

But I was determined to trust God and not worry.

The day I mailed the check, I sat in a park, saying, "Lord, I know that somehow You will provide. I know You have never forsaken me before, and You won't start now."

That night I had the best sleep ever. As was my custom after classes, the next morning I went to my university mailbox. There was large envelope from a friend whose wedding I had performed a few weeks earlier. It contained this note:

> *To many people the number 13 is bad,*
> *but it is our favorite number.*
> *Thank you for performing a great wedding.*

In Australia, where I had ministered during the mid-seventies, a twenty-dollar honorarium for a wedding was a huge thing, and I had made a rule of passing the payment on to the church.

Much to my surprise, however, this envelope contained thirteen one-hundred-dollar bills!

This was God's provision, pure and simple. Now that I am back in the pastorate full-time, I accept no honorarium for ministry of any kind. But back then the message was clear: if I live in obedience, God will provide for my needs.

YOU CAN TAKE GOD'S PROMISES TO THE BANK

The certainty that God keeps His promises is what makes worry a sin.

Suppose I promise my son, "Tomorrow I will give you ten dollars." That means tomorrow he has every right to come to me and say, "May I have my ten dollars now, Dad?" If he stays up all night worrying whether he is going to get the money or not, there is something wrong in our relationship. He has not understood that I am trustworthy.

There is no one more trustworthy than God. What He promises, He delivers. It is wrong to live in a state of worry and anxiety, because God has already committed Himself to give us what we need—if we live in obedience to Him. Not only is worrying wrong, but it ruins our quality of life.

Don't let your effectiveness today be undermined by your fears of what may happen tomorrow. God's promises are firm:

"I tell you the truth," Jesus said to them, "no one who has left home or wife or brothers or parents or children for the sake of the kingdom of God will fail to receive many times as much in this age and, in the age to come, eternal life." (Luke 18:29 NIV)

Our Lord commits Himself irrevocably to taking care of those who put everything on the line for Him. Notice that sense of order again. When you put Him first, He provides for your needs. When He is number-one priority with you—your needs are number-one priority with Him.

I think this principle even applies at the national level.

GOD LOOKS AFTER A CHRISTIAN NATION

I am convinced that the underlying cause of famine and hunger in the world is not bad agricultural policy or overpopulation, though certainly these aggravate the problem. Only 15 percent of the world's arable land is used for agriculture—and that for only half the year. Technical problems of food production can be solved. Far more difficult to root out, however, is the spiritual problem that results in shortages.

Where a country has no Christian roots, there is a tendency to place a low value on human life. In the East, where Hindu beliefs breed fatalism, disease and starvation are sometimes seen as divine punishment, or *karma*. By the logic of the religion, relieving poverty may be wrong because it prevents a person from doing correct penance for past sins. In other belief systems your poverty may be seen as the will of God, and something you dare not challenge.

One reason Western Europe and North America are blessed by God with an abundance of food is that our roots and beliefs are still essentially Christian. Whether the revisionist liberals admit it or not, the idea that God wants to see needs met in a life of obedience has profoundly influenced our productivity. And that Christian foundation should not be lightly cast away.

I fear for countries like America when I see our current leaders ignoring Christian values, when I see an infatuation with Eastern mysticism, and when I see the growing demand for abortion and euthanasia. In indulging our freedoms we are reverting to paganism and forfeiting the blessings of God.

How, then, should we expect God to provide?

GOD'S PROVISION COMES IN THE PRESENT TENSE

God sometimes provides for His children through miraculous intervention. I know, because I have seen it myself. But we should not make the mistake of thinking that trust in God means sitting on our behinds and waiting for our empty plates to fill with food and our empty wallets to fill with dollar bills. They won't!

Most often, God provides for His children by giving them the opportunity to work hard. Paul told the Thessalonian Christians to earn a living, and he added that anyone who refused to do that had no right to eat. God has already provided every one of us with life, energy, resources, intelligence, and opportunities to use these in a job.

And those incapable of working? Most often, God provides for them through the generosity of His people. For on those whom God gives the opportunity to earn, He also lays the duty to give.

Also remember, Jesus told us to pray "Give us *today* our daily bread." He did not tell us to ask for bread we think is due to us from the past. Nor did he lead us to expect that God would provide today what we need tomorrow.

When He dropped manna in the wilderness for the people of Israel, He dropped just enough for their daily needs. People who went out and stockpiled a week's supply found it had gone rotten by the following morning.

Three thousand years later, it is a lesson we can still learn from. When we ask God to give us "our daily bread"—and if we ask it sincerely striving to live a life of obedience—He will give us exactly what we ask for. No more, no less.

PRAYER WORKBOOK

TO REFLECT ON:

As a starting point, think about two needs you have recently brought to God in prayer. They may be very fundamental needs, or very small ones. What would you like God to do for you? I have written two of my needs. Write yours in the spaces that follow.

MY ANSWERS

1. A job for one of our children.
2. Healing for a very dear and precious family friend.

YOUR ANSWERS

1. _____

2. _____
   _____

Write down how God answered or is answering the prayers you listed in the previous section. If God has not answered these prayers, take a look at your spiritual life. Nobody does God's will all of the time, and most of us have some areas where we find obedience particularly difficult. Could there be a link between your willingness to commit your whole life to God and God's readiness to meet these needs? How will you plan to make a special effort to obey God in relation to these needs?

MY ANSWERS

1. God answered, but the job was not in the city we wanted.
2. God has not yet fully answered our prayers, but the friend is improving every day.

YOUR ANSWERS

1. _____

2. _____
_____

TO READ:
Spend a few minutes quietly reflecting on these Scriptures:

When the dew was gone, thin flakes like frost on the ground appeared on the desert floor. When the Israelites saw it, they said to each other, "What is it?" For they did not know what it was.

Moses said to them, "It is the bread the LORD has given you to eat. This is what the LORD has commanded. 'Each one is to gather as much as he needs. Take an omer for each person you have in your tent.'"

The Israelites did as they were told; some gathered much, some little. And when they measured it by the omer, he who gathered much did not have too much, and he who gathered little did not have too little. Each one gathered as much as he needed. (Ex. 16:14–18 NIV)

If that is how God clothes the grass of the field, which is here today and tomorrow is thrown into the fire, will he not much more clothe you, O you of little faith? So do not worry, saying, "What shall we eat?" or "What shall we drink?" or "What shall we wear?" For the pagans run after all these things, and your heavenly Father knows that you need them. But seek first his kingdom and his righteousness, and all these things will be given to you as well. (Matt. 6:30–33 NIV)

> Go to the ant, you sluggard;
>> consider its ways and be wise!
> It has no commander,
>> no overseer or ruler,
> yet it stores its provisions in summer
>> and gathers its food at harvest. (Prov. 6:6–8 NIV)

TO PRAY:

Finally, take a legal pad. Collect all your thoughts and write a prayer that relates what you will do for God (your obedience) to what God will do for you (His provision). As before, try to avoid using "stock phrases." Make sure that everything you thank God for, and everything you ask Him for, comes from your heart and has meaning for you personally. Make the prayer as long or as short as you wish. When you are satisfied with it, copy it into this book. Then spend a little time quietly in the presence of your heavenly Father before speaking it out loud. This is my prayer. Write yours in the space that follows.

MY PRAYER

Father, You are my provider. You have already blessed me with all of my daily necessities. I acknowledge today that every good thing I have comes from Your hand. You, Father, give me strength every morning to work and provide for my family.

I am truly thankful today that all of my daily needs, whether they be physical, emotional, spiritual, or mental, are the subject of Your concern.

Thank You, Father, that You have promised through Scripture that when I seek Your kingdom and righteousness, all of my needs will be met by Your generous providence.

Father, help me today not to take Your provision for granted. Above all, I pray for those who do not have their daily necessities. May they come to know that the secret of Your provision is in the seeking of your kingdom and Your righteousness.

May all Christian people know today that if You care for the birds of the air and the lilies of the field, You will care far more for our needs. Help me today to be conscious of the fine line between need and greed.

YOUR PRAYER

"Forgive Us . . . As We Also Have Forgiven"

8

Forgive and Be Forgiven

A number of years ago a fellow minister, one who did not believe in the divinity of Christ, denounced me publicly for my biblical orthodoxy. It was a painful episode, because he was a prominent clergyman, and we had many friends and associates in common. He was also a very nice guy. But when he saw how firmly I stood in the belief that salvation is by faith in Jesus Christ alone, he became my enemy. "Nobody believes that stuff anymore," he told me.

I tried to reach out to him after that, but in vain. And then one day I saw him at a luncheon. We had both been invited to be part of a steering committee for a citywide function. As I ate my meal that day, I looked around the room. I spotted him at a table with other clergy who did not believe that the Bible was the authoritative Word of God, and who did not believe that Jesus is the only way to heaven. Most of them did not believe in a literal heaven or hell; instead they believed in universal salvation. *So why do they want to be part of an evangelistic campaign?* I wondered.

I was not convinced that I could serve with them on the steering committee. I decided to decline the invitation.

As I was leaving the luncheon, however, I went over to speak to this man who had become my enemy. I bore him no personal animosity; we simply had nothing in common regarding fundamental issues of the faith. Now, I did not believe for a moment that he was a true brother in Christ—nevertheless, I went up to him in front of many of his friends, and threw my arms around him.

I tell you, it was like hugging a street lamp! He stood as stiff as a plank, hands in his pockets—and when I released him he turned on his heel, leaving me standing there blankly, like a comedian who has forgotten his lines. It was mortifying.

I looked like an idiot, I thought as I got in my car.

For the whole drive back home I kept turning the scene over and over in my mind. Every time I replayed it, Satan reminded me how ridiculous I had looked. Gradually I became more and more angry. After all, I had only done what the Bible told me to. It made me pretty sore that God allowed me to be humiliated when I had only been trying to do His will.

Only when I got home to the privacy of my study did I hear what God was saying to me—and look again at what Jesus really taught about forgiving.

THE FORGIVING RIDDLE

The first thing I noticed was how Jesus did not pull any punches. The Lord drew my attention to this passage in Matthew 18. Read it carefully.

> Then Peter came to Jesus and asked, "Lord, how many times shall I forgive my brother when he sins against me? Up to seven times?"
>
> Jesus answered, "I tell you, not seven times, but seventy-seven times.
>
> "Therefore the kingdom of heaven is like a king who wanted to settle accounts with his servants. As he began the settlement, a man who owed him ten thousand talents was brought to him. Since he was not able to pay, the master ordered that he and his wife and his children and all that he had be sold to repay the debt.

"The servant fell on his knees before him. 'Be patient with me,' he begged, 'and I will pay back everything.' The servant's master took pity on him, canceled the debt and let him go.

"But when that servant went out, he found one of his fellow servants who owed him a hundred denarii. He grabbed him and began to choke him. 'Pay back what you owe me!' he demanded.

"His fellow servant fell on his knees and begged him, 'Be patient with me, and I will pay you back.'

"But he refused. Instead, he went off and had the man thrown into prison until he could pay the debt. When the other servants saw what had happened, they were greatly distressed and went and told their master everything that had happened.

"Then the master called the servant in. 'You wicked servant,' he said, 'I canceled all that debt of yours because you begged me to. Shouldn't you have had mercy on your fellow servant just as I had on you?' In anger his master turned him over to the jailers to be tortured until he should pay back all he owed.

"This is how my heavenly Father will treat each one of you unless you forgive your brother from your heart." (Matt. 18:21–35 NIV)

The parable answers a question.

Peter knew patience was a virtue. But he also thought you could have too much of it. Exactly how many times, he wanted to know, does someone have to provoke you before you are free to punch him in the nose?

No doubt he suggested "up to seven times?" thinking this was absurdly generous. Simon Peter would have made a tough judge. Three strikes—and you were definitely out!

But Jesus' reply is uncompromising. Peter must forgive his brother not seven, but seventy-seven times—which means, in effect, as many times as it takes. You do not limit your forgiveness. Fail to forgive others, and you risk severe censure. And there is to be no fibbing, either. Peter must forgive his sinning brother "from the heart."

The parable awakens our sense of natural justice. Nobody hearing it could fail to identify the unforgiving servant as a rascal of the worst kind. We enjoy seeing the tables turned on him at the end. The message is clear: *When God forgives you, He lays on you a solemn duty to forgive others.*

Christians, though, sometimes get muddled about forgiving—and particularly about the role forgiving behavior plays in their own salvation.

FORGIVING IS A SIGN, NOT A PAYMENT

I want to emphasize an important point.

The line in the Lord's Prayer that says "Forgive us our debts, as we also have forgiven our debtors" does *not* mean we earn God's forgiveness by forgiving other people. If that were true, salvation would rest on good works, and faith would be unnecessary.

Paul says, "It is by grace you have been saved, through faith—and this not from yourselves, it is the gift of God—not by works, so that no one can boast" (Eph. 2:8 NIV).

Let's be completely clear about this. Our eternal debt is paid on the cross once and for all. Nothing outstanding. No going back. Vindictive and unforgiving scoundrels are welcome in the kingdom of heaven—so long as they repent and receive new life in Christ. Pious souls who forgive fifty times a day—and think that this alone guarantees them a place—will end up being disappointed. You do not gain entry to heaven by having a great spiritual résumé.

Forgiving others is not a payment—it's a sign of life. Once you have received God's forgiveness of sin in Jesus Christ, and the Holy Spirit has begun to live in your heart, it follows that you should become a more forgiving person.

A willingness to forgive is:

- one of the signs that you belong to the Lord Jesus Christ

- one of the signs that God is your Father and that the Holy Spirit dwells in you

- one of the signs that you have the divine nature working inside you

Christians do not forgive one another out of duty, or in order to "score points." They do it to express thanksgiving to God and to make His heart glad. We should start *wanting* to forgive others, even when we find it very hard to do, and even when actual reconciliation seems well nigh impossible, because joining the family of our heavenly Father gives us a desire to emulate Him, to follow in Jesus' footsteps.

That is our privilege. And the more we exercise it, the more the Spirit will help us and transform us.

KEEP YOUR FEET CLEAN!

After my disastrous attempt to show forgiveness to someone who set himself to be my enemy, God showed me a second passage in the Gospels—this one from John 13:

Jesus knew that the Father had put all things under his power, and that he had come from God and was returning to God; so he got up from the meal, took off his outer clothing, and wrapped a towel round his waist. After that, he poured water into a basin and began to wash his disciples' feet, drying them with the towel that was wrapped around him.

He came to Simon Peter, who said to him, "Lord, are you going to wash my feet?"

Jesus replied, "You do not realize now what I am doing, but later you will understand."

"No," said Peter, "you shall never wash my feet."

Jesus answered, "Unless I wash you, you have no part with me."

"Then, Lord," Simon Peter replied, "not just my feet but my hands and my head as well!"

Jesus answered, "A person who has had a bath needs only to wash his feet; his whole body is clean. And you are clean, though not every one of you." For he knew who was going to betray him, and that was why he said not every one was clean. (vv. 3–11 NIV)

I saw at once that I have a lot in common with Peter!

He did not want the Lord to wash his feet. Like me, he felt much more comfortable doing things for others than having others do things for him. In addition, it scandalized him to think of Jesus the Messiah doing a job normally associated with the lowest of the low. He resisted and began to argue.

So Jesus had to spell things out to Peter in no uncertain terms. "Unless I wash you," He said, "you are not my disciple."

Tough talk! And immediately Peter caved in. If his salvation was at stake, he would willingly strip off so Jesus could wash him from head to toe.

And then Jesus said this: "A person who has had a bath needs only to wash his feet; his whole body is clean."

What did He mean?

Well, simply that there is a difference between repentance for the sinner and repentance for the believer.

The first time we come to God and ask forgiveness for our sins, we are spiritually bathed and disinfected. From that moment on, we are basically clean. All our previous sins have been showered off and washed down the drain, never to return. Nothing we can do will bring them back, or reduce us to the same abject state of dirtiness we were in before we came to Christ.

At the same time, says Jesus, even clean people cannot avoid getting a little dust on their feet. Much as they may desire to stay absolutely pure, all Christians continue to commit sins. And while these new sins will never endanger a believer's salvation, they can, if left unattended, reduce him or her to a life of unfulfilled and miserable compromise. You can be a Christian and still have stinky feet!

That is why many church services begin with an act of corporate confession. It's not so we can all be saved again. Rather, it's to let us "wash the street dust off our feet" before we enter God's house. A modern equivalent would be washing your car before going on a trip.

We confess our latest sins to God, so that God can cleanse us. If we do not confess them, these sins hang around, inhibiting our relationship with God and spoiling our joy and fulfillment.

The Bible lays out the alternatives clearly.

On the one hand, "If we confess our sins, he is faithful and just and will forgive us our sins and purify us from all unrighteousness" (1 John 1:9 NIV). But on the other hand, "He who conceals his sins does not prosper" (Prov. 28:13 NIV).

And here we come back to the Lord's Prayer.

For in this regular pattern of prayer, we find a formula for confessing our sins and receiving that daily "foot-washing" from Jesus.

Except it carries a heavy reminder.

True, forgiveness for the salvation of our souls is freely given—graciously offered with no conditions and no probation period. But once saved, we cannot breeze into God's presence and ask to be forgiven for our most recent sins, *if we have not been willing to extend this same courtesy to others.*

"Forgive us our debts, *as we also have forgiven* our debtors."

FORGIVING SELDOM COMES EASY

There are two sides to forgiving:

- transforming your attitude toward the person who has offended you
- transforming your relationship with the person who has offended you

Both take guts.

The first takes guts because—let's face it—we much prefer to go on clinging to our resentments. That way we have a scapegoat. When things go wrong, we can say, "Well, that's because of So-and-So and the awful thing he did to me."

It's childish, yet we find the habit incredibly hard to break. Most of the time the best we manage is to "forgive but not forget"—which is no good at all, because "not forgetting" reserves our right to bring the matter up again whenever we please.

Real forgiveness has no memory. It does not shut other people into the locker of their own past mistakes. It makes room for a genuine fresh start.

Often this transformation of attitude is all you need to transform the relationship. Other times, though, getting a relationship back on track takes a more proactive approach—and that also takes guts.

That is what I was trying to do when I confronted the man who had denounced me. I tell you, it hurt! When the person you are trying to forgive piles insult on top of injury, you are soon tempted to give up.

Getting back to the privacy of my own study later that night, I fell to my knees and said to God, "Don't You realize how idiotic I looked?"

"Sure, you looked like an idiot," I sensed God reply.

"Then why do You have to make it so hard for me?" I complained.

And then I felt God answer: "And don't you think My Son looked like an idiot, when He hung on the cross for your sins?"

It was then I gained a new depth of insight into what it cost Jesus to die for my sins.

Usually we think of the crucifixion in terms of pain—the sheer physical agony of having iron nails driven through your hands and feet. But there was a whole different side to it. The nakedness. The stripping away of dignity. The humiliation and ridicule. "Feeling like an idiot" does not come anywhere close.

In any circumstances, forgiving is a difficult and painful business. Because forgiving always involves "taking a hit"—reaching out with no guarantee that the other person will respond. That was difficult for God the Son. It will be doubly difficult for us.

And I'll tell you why.

DITCH THAT PROUD HEART

In the middle of the worship service, a pastor always called the children forward to give them a children's message. This particular Sunday he was teaching about forgiving one another. He was taking a bit of a risk, actually.

"Yesterday somebody said something that hurt me very much," he said to the children. "That person said I spent too much time thinking about myself. That really upset me. Now, do you think I ought to forgive that person, or not?"

You can usually rely on a preacher's child to come up with the right answer. Sure enough, it was his own six-year-old daughter who put her hand up. "Yes, you should," she said.

"But why?" the pastor asked. "That person said something I think is untrue and really hurt my feelings. Why should I just forgive?"

And without a moment's hesitation, his young daughter replied, "Because you are married to her."

The child, of course, had seen right to the heart of the issue.

God is perfect. He has no hang-ups or insecurities. And so when He forgives a sinner, He does it purely with the sinner's good in mind.

We are rather less perfect than God. Even the best of us has a fragile ego. And when we try to forgive others, we are not only thinking of them. We're thinking of us—of our punctured self-image and damaged credibility.

Because we feel vulnerable, we see *not forgiving* others as a way to save face and avoid being trampled on. To protect ourselves, we withdraw. We define ourselves as victims—innocent people on whom injuries have been inflicted. In other words, hidden underneath our reluctance to forgive others is that tired old sin of pride.

This readiness to keep old hurts in circulation has had profound consequences. Few things short-circuit the power of the Church of Jesus Christ like unresolved conflict among its members. Few things cripple our effectiveness for Christ in the world like harboring resentments and being unable to shake off past bitterness.

Pride can wreck any relationship. With brothers and sisters, with colleagues and coworkers. It's lethal. And once you've started letting pride have its way, it's very hard to stop. I have met adults who still nurse resentments against their parents—twenty years after their parents have died.

WHOSE SIDE ARE YOU ON?

Yet forgiving lies at the heart of the gospel. It should be a litmus test separating those who are committed to Christ from those who are not. When you forgive, you follow the example of Jesus; when you harbor bitterness and resentment, you follow the example of Satan.

Because Satan never forgives. The very name *Satan* means "adversary." The Bible calls him the "accuser" of Christians. When Satan sees forgiveness, he does his utmost to undo and spoil it.

So when someone takes advantage of you, when someone lets you down, when someone speaks ill of you—you have a choice. You can act like Satan, the accuser. Or you can manifest the divine nature that became yours the day you said yes to Jesus.

Few things please the heart of God more than a readiness to forgive. At such moments God sees His image and likeness in us. And that's why, when you truly forgive another person, a deep peace floods your heart. It's like being let out of prison.

But do not expect all forgiveness to work instantaneously—sometimes you will have to work at it.

FORGIVENESS IS A PROCESS

We would all like forgiveness to be a first-round, knock-out punch. But there are two situations in which it can go the whole fifteen rounds.

First—we may as well be honest!—if someone hurts us once, he or she will probably hurt us again. That is particularly true of those we are close to, because the closer you are to someone, the more opportunities you have to annoy each other. In that sort of situation, forgiving is a long-term project and needs careful daily management.

Second, of course, forgiving is a skill we acquire with practice. It was Charles Spurgeon, the "prince of preachers," who once said, "Cultivate forbearance until your heart yields a fine crop of it. Pray for a short memory as to unkindness."

When we have been hurt, our first instinct is to nurse the wound with bitterness. That is a mistake. Treat a mental wound that way, and it will continue to fester. Five years down the road it will still be painful to you.

The only way to heal a hurt caused by someone else's thoughtlessness or unkindness is to hit right back—by forgiving. Forgiveness is the salve that keeps a wound free of infection and allows it to heal. Forgiving is good for you. It makes you well again.

Of course, you don't have to go to the Bible to find that advice; modern psychology has discovered it too. But psychology does not give you the strength to make forgiveness real. Only God can do that. When forgiving requires more strength than we possess, we have the power of the Father, the example of the Son, and the strength of the Spirit to help us.

So the next time you pray, put forgiveness into action. Is there anyone you feel alienated from? Someone who makes you tense up, causes your pulse to beat a little faster?

Then give yourself a test. Ask God to pour out the riches of His blessing on that person's life.

Can you do that with enthusiasm? Or do you feel you're just going through the motions? If you cannot ask God to bless someone—and mean it wholeheartedly—you probably have some forgiving to do.

I suggest that you start right now.

PRAYER
WORKBOOK

TO REFLECT ON:

As a starting point, think about your experience of being forgiven by God. As a Christian you will know that God has wiped away your sins and brought you into His kingdom. You will also come to God regularly, confessing that you need to "wash your feet" and seek His cleansing. Try to think of two ways in which being forgiven by God changes your outlook, attitude, and actions. I have written down two things that have changed for me. Put your answers in the spaces that follow.

MY ANSWERS

1. I see people in the way I looked at God before Christ came into my life.
2. I put myself in their place, so I can understand their hurts and the reasons they react the way they do.

YOUR ANSWERS

1. _____

2. _____

Now think about the people you have most trouble forgiving. In light of what you have learned from the Lord's Prayer, work out two things you can do that will help you forgive them and make that forgiveness effective over the long term. Ask yourself not only how you intend to make a permanent change in your attitudes, but how those attitudes will find expression in the way you behave.

MY ANSWERS

1. I pray for an opportunity where they need my help so that I can prove to them that they are forgiven.
2. I write notes and tell them that I am praying for them.

YOUR ANSWERS

1. _____

   _____

2. _____

   _____

TO READ:

Spend a few minutes quietly reflecting on these Scriptures:

> In my anguish I cried to the LORD,
>> and he answered by setting me free.
> The LORD is with me; I will not be afraid.
>> What can man do to me? (Ps. 118:5–6 NIV)

[Jesus said,] "You have heard that it was said, 'Love your neighbor and hate your enemy.' But I tell you: Love your enemies and pray for those who persecute you, that you may be sons of your Father in heaven. He causes his sun to rise on the evil and the good, and sends rain on the righteous and the unrighteous. If you love those who love you, what reward will you get? Are not even the tax collectors doing that? And if you greet only your brothers, what are you doing more than others? Do not even pagans do that? Be perfect, therefore, as your heavenly Father is perfect." (Matt. 5:43–48 NIV)

Therefore, as God's chosen people, holy and dearly loved, clothe yourselves with compassion, kindness, humility, gentleness and patience. Bear with each other and forgive whatever grievances you may have against one another. Forgive as the Lord forgave you. And over all these virtues put on love, which binds them all together in perfect unity.

Let the peace of Christ rule in your hearts, since as members of one body you were called to peace. And be thankful. (Col. 3:12–15 NIV)

TO PRAY:

Finally, take a legal pad. Collect all your thoughts and write a prayer that expresses your response to the challenge to forgive as the Lord has forgiven you. As before, try to avoid using "stock phrases." Make sure that everything you thank God for, and everything you ask Him for, comes from your heart and has meaning for you personally. Make the prayer as long or as short as you wish. When you are satisfied with it, copy it into this book. Then spend a little time quietly in the presence of your heavenly Father before speaking it out loud. This is my prayer. Write yours in the space that follows.

MY PRAYER

Father, thank You that I am forgiven, and that nothing can now stand between me and Your eternal love. All my past sins have been blotted out and will never return.

Father, I want to forgive others as You have forgiven me. I want to forgive, and also forget. Forgive me for the times I hold onto my resentments. Forgive me for the times I have enjoyed having someone to blame. Release me from this "victim mentality" and give me strength to move forward.

Help me to transform my attitude when people do things to hurt me. May I not make enemies of them. May I instead find ways of restoring broken relationships, and communicating my forgiveness in a constructive way.

Father, You are Lord in all my relationships. Give me Your Spirit's strength to deal with the human pride that makes forgiveness so hard. And give me Your Son's determination to go on forgiving, even when forgiving is hard and painful.

Most of all, Father, may I be able to forgive in the relationships that are most important to me. May I always be able to see the pressures other people live and work under. May I love and support them in difficult times, and be an example of the forgiving love of Your Son, Jesus.

YOUR PRAYER

"Lead Us Not into Temptation"

9

Put Yourself Beyond Satan's Reach

Now we come to the most controversial line in the Lord's Prayer. So far we have looked at:

- the privilege of being in God's family: "our Father"

- the promise of living with God for eternity: "in heaven"

- the joy of belonging to God: "hallowed be Your name"

- the transformation of citizenship with God: "Your kingdom come"

- the determination to obey God: "Your will be done"

- the peace of dependence on God: "Give us today our daily bread"

- the challenge of imitating God: "Forgive us our debts, as we also have forgiven our debtors"

And now comes: "Lead us not into temptation."

This line has caused a storm of controversy because nobody can agree on what it means. After all, when we pray these words, we seem to imply that God is trying to make us sin. Can that be true?

This question has plagued theologians for nearly two thousand years. It seems impossible that a pure and sinless God would want His children to disobey Him. Far more likely, we lead ourselves into temptation. And yet Jesus did not tell us to pray, "Give us the good sense to avoid sinning."

So what does it mean to pray, "Lead us not into temptation"?

ARE WE TESTED OR TEMPTED?

At the root of the question is a muddle about New Testament Greek. Look, for example, at these two passages from the same chapter in James:

> Consider it pure joy, my brothers, whenever you face trials of many kinds, because you know that the testing of your faith develops perseverance. Perseverance must finish its work so that you may be mature and complete, not lacking anything . . . Blessed is the man who perseveres under trial, because when he has stood the test, he will receive the crown of life that God has promised to those who love him. (James 1:2–4, 12 NIV)

> When tempted, no one should say, "God is tempting me." For God cannot be tempted by evil, nor does he tempt anyone; but each one is tempted when, by his own evil desire, he is dragged away and enticed. Then, after desire has conceived, it gives birth to sin; and sin, when it is full-grown, gives birth to death. (James 1:13–15 NIV)

Testing, said James, will do you good. When you're tested, you learn to persevere, and you become mature and complete. People who pass the test receive a heavenly reward.

Temptation, on the other hand, is an unmitigated evil. Rooted in a person's "evil desire," it drags him down as surely as testing will pull him up. It lets desire blossom into sin, and sin blossom into death.

Not surprisingly, James told us that God has no part in temptation. God can neither tempt nor be tempted. On the other hand—though James did not say it in so many words—testing seems to happen with God's permission. We are to rejoice in our trials because they aid our progress toward perfection.

As different kinds of "tough experience," then, testing and temptation would appear to be almost diametrical opposites.

But now let me tell you a strange thing. *Testing* and *temptation* are translations of the same word in New Testament Greek.

That word, *peirasmos,* can be used positively or negatively. It can mean testing or enticing. It can mean seduction to evil, or a revealing of one's moral character. It can imply corruption, or the bringing of good out of bad.

So when we pray, "Lead us not into temptation," we are saying to God, "Please don't put me in a situation where I might fail You."

Because you can be sure of this: what the Greeks called *peirasmos* lies at the cutting edge of Christian discipleship.

WHAT GOD AND SATAN ARE DOING WHEN YOU ARE TEMPTED

Let me give you an illustration to help you understand the subtle but crucial distinction inherent in this concept of *peirasmos.*

The builders of the Union Pacific Railroad once had to construct an elaborate trestle bridge across a large canyon. Civil engineering was a less sophisticated affair in those days. People had no detailed knowledge of materials, nor were there any computers on hand to model stress patterns in different bridge designs. The engineer built the bridge as best he knew how—and then tried it out.

When the UPR engineer had completed this particular trestle bridge, he loaded a train with enough extra cars and equipment to double its normal payload. Then he drove it out to the middle of the bridge and left it there for an entire day.

"Are you trying to break this bridge?" someone asked him.

"No," replied the engineer, "I am trying to prove that the bridge will not break."

In spiritual terms this illustrates a vital distinction.

Putting the weight of the overloaded train on the bridge is *peirasmos*. The bridge suffers stress. It may break—or it may prove strong enough to withstand the pressure.

Hidden behind this reality, though, are two contrasting motives.

God is like the engineer. His motive in letting us experience *peirasmos* is not to see whether we will break, but to let us prove we will not. For exactly the same reason, He sent his own Son into the wilderness to be tempted by Satan. "Jesus, full of the Holy Spirit, returned from the Jordan and was led by the Spirit in the desert, where for forty days he was tempted by the devil" (Luke 4:1–2 NIV). Remember that: Satan did not lure Jesus into the desert; God's Spirit led him there, knowing full well what was about to happen.

Satan's motive, on the other hand, is purely destructive. He hopes that the *peirasmos* will prove our undoing. He takes every opportunity to pummel us, wanting to break us and drive us to evil.

So, in the very same situation, Satan tempts us—and God tests us.

- Satan's intention is to bring us down; God's intention is to strengthen us and mature us.

- Satan's intention is to defeat us; God's intention is for us to appropriate His power and win.

- Satan's intention is to discourage us; God's intention is to lift us above discouragement.

- Satan's intention is to make us feel bad about ourselves; God's intention is to make us feel great about our heavenly Daddy.

- Satan's intention is to make us cater to self; God's intention is for us to bring honor and glory to His name.

THREE KEY FACTS ABOUT TEMPTATION

Here are three very important facts about temptation.

1. Satan has freedom to attack you. Since the Fall, Satan has been given a limited and temporary freedom to act against the will of God. The Bible does not tell us all the limits of this freedom, though it does imply that Satan cannot try us without God's permission.

Look carefully, for instance, at Peter's betrayal of Jesus at the crucifixion. Jesus warned him beforehand: "Simon, Simon, Satan has asked to sift you as wheat. But I have prayed for you, Simon, that your faith may not fail. And when you have turned back, strengthen your brothers" (Luke 22:31–32 NIV).

With Peter, Satan was allowed to go only so far and no farther. The same sort of thing happened with Job, where we see Satan going before God's throne and challenging God to test Job by destroying his livelihood. There again, God leaves the tempting to Satan: "Very well, then, everything he has is in your hands, but on the man himself do not lay a finger" (Job 1:12 NIV).

2. Satan knows where your weak points are. Take note how Peter reacted to Jesus' warning. "But he replied, 'Lord, I am ready to go with you to prison and to death'" (Luke 22:33 NIV).

Satan has good intelligence. He knows exactly which areas of our lives are not fully under the control of the Holy Spirit—and he zeros in on them with bull's-eye accuracy.

Did Peter's behavior measure up to his bravado? Hardly! He fled under the gentlest of questioning from mere bystanders at Jesus' trial. He even denied he knew Jesus. And why? Because Satan had identified Peter's weak spot. He knew Peter valued nothing more than his own skin, and he made sure to put Peter in just the situation he was least equipped to deal with.

Result: Satan 1, Peter 0.

Don't think you're any different!

Who has the upper hand in the various areas of your life? You—or God?

Does God rule supreme when it comes to things like fear, insecurity, worry, anger, unforgiveness, lust, lying, addiction, greed?

If you are in control—in any of these or other areas—then praying "lead us not into temptation" will not help you one bit. By refusing to let God in, you have already given access to Satan. Nothing will protect you from him. You have switched off the burglar alarm and thrown the doors wide open.

3. Once you see temptation coming, it's already too late. We usually pray most earnestly against temptation when temptation is already upon us. Like the fat man who accidentally drove past the pastry shop, we feel its pull in the same way an object in space feels the pull of a black hole. The closer we get, the more powerfully it sucks us in.

The trick is not to get too close. In that way, "Lead us not into temptation" is similar to "Your kingdom come." Both ask God to do something—and in both cases the prayer bounces back with a challenge to our own behavior.

Do you really want to beat Satan? Then let's look carefully at how temptation works.

STEP ONE: SNEAK IN UNDER THE RADAR

In one of Charles Shultz's *Peanuts* cartoons, the children have to write an essay telling how they feel about returning to school after the summer break.

In her essay Lucy writes: "Vacations are nice, but it is good to be back to school. There is nothing more satisfying or challenging than education, and I look forward to a year of expanding my knowledge."

Needless to say, this gets a warm commendation from the teacher.

In the final frame, a smiling Lucy leans over to Charlie Brown and confides, "After a while you learn what sells."

There is something of Satan in Lucy! For Satan also knows what sells. He has done his market research. In fact, he figured out what made humanity tick the first time he turned up in the Garden of Eden.

It is worth studying Satan's method. Because the good news is that he is not very original. He has found a formula, and he uses it again and again. So understand how it works, and you won't fall for it so easily.

Did Satan sidle up to Eve and say, "Hi, I'm Satan. I'm here to make you disobey God"?

No way.

The last thing Satan wants to do is set alarm bells ringing. So he starts in by persuading us to turn off the sensors. He confuses that whole mechanism inside us that makes a clear distinction between right and wrong.

"Now the serpent was more crafty than any of the animals the LORD God had made. He said to the woman, 'Did God really say, "You must not eat from any tree in the garden"?'" (Gen. 3:1 NIV)

Subtly he introduced the thought that God might be unreasonable—that He might have placed off-limits not just the Tree of Knowledge of Good and Evil, but the entire orchard. And Eve played ball. She made the mistake of entering into dialogue, discussing with the serpent what it was God "really said."

Long before he can get a temptation to stick, Satan will do his spadework by making you doubt the authority of the Word of God. He will muddy your interpretation. He will suggest that you are taking one of a number of possible angles on the text. He will argue that it is impossible to live by the Word of God when so little agreement exists on what it actually says.

And then, in place of the clear teaching of the Word, Satan will feed you other, unbiblical ideas that our modern age finds more palatable:

- the idea that biblical teaching cannot be expected to apply to our modern, sophisticated age

- the idea that as long as you don't hurt anyone you can pretty much do what you want

- the idea that the Old Testament God, so obviously irritable and unstable, gave way in the New Testament to another kind of God whose watchword was *love* and who tolerates almost any kind of behavior you could describe with the word *liberal*

And now that your security system has been neutralized, Satan moves on to the second step.

STEP TWO: USE A FAT WORM

No angler worth his salt will dangle a hook in the water and hope the fish will bite. Fish are not stupid. But they *are* hungry—and greedy. And if the angler sinks his hook into just the right kind of juicy, appetizing worm, the fish will bite.

This is where Satan puts his intelligence about you to such good use. He has a bag full of your very favorite worms. And he has threaded every one of them onto a barbed and dangerous hook. No sooner, then, did Eve pick up the discussion about what God "really said," than Satan turned into a salesman.

> "'You will not surely die,' the serpent said to the woman. 'For God knows that when you eat of it your eyes will be opened, and you will be like God, knowing good and evil'" (Gen. 3:4–5 NIV).

Satan supplied no proof in support of this assertion about God's motives. But that didn't matter. Eve's attention was shifted onto the worm—and a very attractive worm it was. She was only a nibble away from becoming exactly like God, Satan told her. All she had to do was pick that fruit and eat.

Of course, the tempter knew Eve inside out. Once he had gotten her attention, he knew he could pretty much take it to the bank. He concentrated on the benefits. He purred about her self-fulfillment. He emphasized how happy she would be—and who turns down the chance to be happy? It took only a few, well-chosen words. Eve's imagination did the rest.

> When the woman saw that the fruit of the tree was good for food and pleasing to the eye, and also desirable for gaining wisdom, she took some and ate it. She also gave some to her husband, who was with her, and he ate it. (Gen. 3:6 NIV)

Note the impact of peer pressure. When Eve fell, Adam tamely followed. Satan knows all about the power of personal recommendation and example. A moment later he had both fish impaled on the same hook.

STEP THREE: ENSURE THAT SINNING IS FUN

But not so fast.

Today we're not in quite the same situation as Adam and Eve. In their case Satan needed only one sin to cause the fall of humankind. Judgment and retribution followed almost immediately.

In our case he slowly gets us hooked. Most of us slip into sin by degrees. Each degree is very small. And the drift into entrapment may take many years to complete. But we fall just as surely as Adam and Eve did.

Satan's temptations almost always begin by focusing on the positives. He gets us to imagine what advantages might come our way if we took a less ethical line. Without actually committing ourselves to evil, we speculate on how things might feel if we *did*.

Once you begin to do that, Satan knows he is halfway there. He has got you mentally sampling the goods. He is beginning to sell you on the dream of having your cake and eating it too, of enjoying the blessings of faith and also the illicit joys of sin.

For it does not bother Satan one bit when we enjoy sinning. That's how he gets us to do it. Unlike Eve, we do not sin once and immediately get stung. We get a high—and we get a habit. Satan's whole strategy revolves around sinking us into dependency. One bite of the fruit is not enough. One look is not enough. One visit is not enough. One drag is not enough. We want more. And we know where to get it.

Once Satan has established a beachhead in your life, he soon secures his position. And the longer he can string you along and keep your cooperation, the more secure he becomes.

By now, praying "lead me not into temptation" will do you as much good as reciting the phone book. Your prayer will be faint and half-hearted. You'll say the words, but you'll mean, "Not now, not today. I need just one more hit."

That's why resisting temptation is so difficult. Just like narcotics, sin is addictive. God could deliver you with a snap of His fingers. But you no longer want to be delivered. You don't want the temptation to completely go away. Your will has been divided.

STEP FOUR: BECOME CONVINCED THAT RESISTANCE IS HOPELESS

A Wall Street broker who had struggled for years with heroin addiction said, "It's only when you start talking about giving it up that you know you're addicted."

Much the same is true with temptation. Sooner or later you admit to yourself that you're in the ditch and you need help. You feel guilty. You feel discouraged. You know you've messed up.

Of course, Satan is still pulling his confidence trick. By the grace and strength of the Holy Spirit, any Christian can absolutely and decisively offer his life to the Lord—at any time. But Satan will try his hardest to stop that.

He will deploy a number of strategies—all of them ways of sapping our will to resist. He will tell you:

- that the situation you're in is your fault, so God won't help you

- that you are beyond forgiveness, so it doesn't matter

- that even if you repent, you'll never have the willpower to see it through

- that since you've already blown it, you may as well keep on sinning and enjoy yourself

Most of all, he will raise the cost of coming clean. He will encourage you to go through the motions of Christian commitment, while living a life of total defeat. He will encourage you to deceive your Christian brothers and sisters and pretend that everything is okay when it patently is not. Such a state of affairs cannot continue for long, however.

Then the eyes of both of them were opened, and they realized they were naked; so they sewed fig leaves together and made coverings for themselves.

Then the man and his wife heard the sound of the LORD God as he was walking in the garden in the cool of the day, and they hid from the LORD God among the trees of the Garden. But the LORD God called to the man, "Where are you?" (Gen. 3:7–9 NIV)

Like Adam and Eve, we sense an underlying separation from our heavenly Father. No amount of sewing fig leaves together or skulking in the undergrowth will change that fact.

We can put up a good Christian front. But deep down we are concealing and rationalizing our defeat. We say all the right things in Sunday school class, but within we know the bitter reality of failure and compromise. We cannot even talk honestly with our heavenly Father, because we have too much to hide.

Our situation differs from that of Adam and Eve in only one respect. Unlike them, we will not be cursed and flung from Paradise. But we will know the depths of despair. For our Christian faith will be like a car with no engine. We will have sat for years at the wheel—and gone nowhere.

Start Fighting Now!

A Christian ensnared by temptation is like the elderly lady who was taken in by a bonanza investment scheme. When she lost everything, she called the Better Business Bureau.

"This was a bogus institution," they told her. "Why didn't you call us first to check it out? Didn't you know about us?"

"I knew all about you," she replied. "But I didn't want to call you—because you would have told me what I didn't want to hear."

God does not lead us into temptation. We lead ourselves into temptation. If we truly want to have victory over Satan, we need to act now—not when Satan already has us in his sights. We need to be willing to listen to what we don't want to hear. We need every part of our lives to be occupied by the Holy Spirit. Try to resist temptation too late—or on your own—and Satan will brush your resistance aside.

God does not want you to be defeated. He wants you to be victorious. Temptation in itself is not evil. It is an endurance test in which Satan's purpose is to break us, and God's purpose is to give us greater strength of character and more Christlike perfection.

From God's standpoint, temptation is a great opportunity. It can help us grow up into godliness under the guidance of the Holy Spirit who dwells within. In his translation of James 1:2–4, J.B. Phillips says that when trials and temptations crowd into your life, you should not resent them as intruders, but welcome them as friends.

No one relishes trials. Even Jesus, in the Garden of Gethsemane, prayed, "My Father, if it is possible, may this cup be taken from me. Yet not as I will, but as you will" (Matt. 26:39 NIV). That is what it means to pray, "Lead us not into temptation."

Yet, as unwelcome as trials and temptations may be, James pointed out that they have a part in God's plan. "Perseverance," he wrote, makes us "mature and complete" (1:4 NIV). Tough experiences make us grow up. Having choices is part of learning to choose wisely. God does not want us to suffer or fail, but He does want us to graduate with honors in the School of Life.

PRAYER
WORKBOOK

TO REFLECT ON:

As a starting point, think about times in the past when you "withstood the tests" you went through. Maybe when you were tempted to do something you knew was wrong, or when you endured a period of hardship. Try to learn some lessons from these experiences. Name two things you did at these times that contributed positively to your success. I have written down two things that have helped me in the past. Put your answers in the spaces that follow.

MY ANSWERS

1. When I had no money, I was tempted to renege on my commitment to give God back what belongs to Him.
2. As a discouraged minister, I was tempted to quit and walk away from serving God's people.

YOUR ANSWERS

1. _____

   _____

2. _____

   _____

Now think of a trial or temptation you are going through at the moment. You want this to be a growing and learning experience, not a defeat. Think of two strategies you will employ over the coming days to ensure that you allow the Holy Spirit into every area of your life, and so strengthen yourself in times of testing.

MY ANSWERS

1. Pray for guidance and courage in making hard decisions.
2. Be careful not to let Satan appeal to my physical tiredness or weakness and thus tempt me into disobedience.

YOUR ANSWERS

1. _____

   _____
2. _____

   _____

TO READ:

Spend a few minutes quietly reflecting on these Scriptures:

Do not merely listen to the word, and so deceive yourselves. Do what it says. Anyone who listens to the word but does not do what it says is like a man who looks at his face in a mirror and, after looking at himself, goes away and immediately forgets what he looks like. But the man who looks intently into the perfect law that gives freedom, and continues to do this, not forgetting what he has heard, but doing it— he will be blessed in what he does. (James 1:22–25 NIV)

Dear friends, do not be surprised at the painful trial you are suffering, as though something strange were happening to you. But rejoice that you participate in the sufferings of Christ, so that you may be over-joyed when his glory is revealed. If you are insulted because of the name of Christ, you are blessed, for the Spirit of glory and of God rests on you. (1 Peter 4:12–14 NIV)

So, if you think you are standing firm, be careful that you don't fall! No temptation has seized you except what is common to man. And God is faithful; he will not let you be tempted beyond what you can bear. But when you are tempted, he will also provide a way out so that you can stand up under it. (1 Cor. 10:12–13 NIV)

TO PRAY:

Finally, take a legal pad. Collect all your thoughts and write a prayer that deals with your experience of testing and temptation. As before, try to avoid using "stock phrases." Make sure that everything you thank God for, and everything you ask Him for, comes from your heart and has meaning for you personally. Make the prayer as long or as short as you wish. When you are satisfied with it, copy it into this book. Then spend a little time quietly in the presence of your heavenly Father before speaking it out loud. This is my prayer. Write yours in the space that follows.

MY PRAYER

Father, I know that Satan is constantly tempting me to sin and disobey You. Father, I further know that You may at times turn Satan's temptation into a test. Testing my loyalty to You and Your word. Testing my commitment to integrity and honesty. Testing my walk and my talk.

Father, let me pass the test with flying colors.

Today let me experience the power of Your victory.

Today help me not to just survive temptation but to thrive on defeating temptation.

Today empower me to be all that You want me to be—whether the temptation is in thought, word, or deed. Give me the will and the strength to be victorious on all fronts.

Remind me that when I go through the test of my own private Gethsemane and my own Good Friday, Easter is just around the corner.

Remind me that You will never test me beyond my ability to bear.

Remind me that with the testing You will open an escape hatch as a way to triumph through obedience and submission.

YOUR PRAYER

"DELIVER US FROM THE EVIL ONE"

10

Avoid Sins of the Human Spirit

I have to begin this chapter by making a confession.

As a leader and a visionary, I sometimes have trouble receiving criticism graciously. On the small things I often hold no opinion. It does not bother me much what computer software we use in the church office, or what arrangements we make for keeping the gardens tidy. But on big issues—issues of doctrine and policy—my convictions are very strong indeed, and criticisms are not readily welcomed.

In one way that's good. You cannot lead effectively unless you have a strong sense of direction. But this quality brings with it corresponding pitfalls. Visionary leadership can easily spill over into pig-headedness, inability to accept good counsel, and a belief that you are always right. For me, it's a daily commitment to keep to the right side of that line. Many times I wait upon the Lord longer than I would like to—just to be sure that I am in His perfect will.

Thankfully, God has placed strong and wise church leaders around me. But I take the matter seriously and make it a frequent subject of prayer, because having too high a regard for your own savvy can get you into deep spiritual trouble.

That's what happened to King David, and it cost an entire nation dearly.

WHY COUNTING YOUR TROOPS IS WRONG

A passage in 1 Chronicles shows how David, one of the most gifted leaders in history, made a huge and avoidable mistake.

> Satan rose up against Israel and incited David to take a census of Israel. So David said to Joab and the commanders of the troops, "Go and count the Israelites from Beersheba to Dan. Then report back to me so that I may know how many there are."
>
> But Joab replied, "May the LORD multiply his troops a hundred times over. My lord the king, are they not all my lord's subjects? Why does my lord want to do this? Why should he bring guilt on Israel?"
>
> The king's word, however, overruled Joab; so Joab left and went throughout Israel and then came back to Jerusalem. Joab reported the number of the fighting men to David: In all Israel there were one million one hundred thousand men who could handle a sword, including four hundred and seventy thousand in Judah.
>
> But Joab did not include Levi and Benjamin in the numbering, because the king's command was repulsive to him. This command was also evil in the sight of God; so he punished Israel.
>
> Then David said to God, "I have sinned greatly by doing this. Now I beg you, take away the guilt of your servant. I have done a very foolish thing." (1 Chron. 21:1–8 NIV)

This is one of two key occasions on which David—normally a shrewd and godly leader—fell headlong into the grossest kind of sin. He had done it once by committing adultery with Bathsheba. Now he did it again by numbering his troops.

You may ask what made this sin so bad. In an age of precision like ours, how many troops are on the army payroll is a basic statistic. And anyway, censuses had been taken in Israel before—notably by Moses in Exodus 30. Why did David's census incur God's wrath?

Here's why: what mattered was not the counting, but the motive.

Moses counted the people because God told him to. After the deliverance from Egypt, every Israelite male of twenty years and up had to pay God a "ransom for his life" (Ex. 30:12 NIV). It was to remind the people that God had brought them out of slavery and would deliver them to the promised land. God commanded, and Moses counted.

But David's case was different. He wanted the census done simply for his own satisfaction. It was like a wealthy man reclining in his leather chair and calculating his net worth—just so he can bask in the warmth of his own glory. Moses had ordered a census out of obedience to God. David ordered a census out of pride.

Behind the scenes, it was Satan's work. And it marked a striking shift in David's attitudes.

Many years before, when he had first seen Goliath, David had asked his fellow Israelites, "Who is this uncircumcised Philistine that he should defy the armies of the living God?" (1 Sam. 17:26 NIV). There was no doubt in David's mind then that the armies belonged to God. But now he had been crowned king—and things were different. He had seen a string of successful campaigns. He was adored by the people. And the high life had started to go to his head.

There is a story about the mule who carried Jesus into Jerusalem. As everyone in the city shouted and threw down their cloaks in front of him, the animal thought, *My, I must be a pretty special mule if people greet me like this!*

For David to take pride in the army of God was no less absurd. It was a very particular form of egotism—an egotism that annexes to itself the rights and privileges of God. And that is not the kind of thing God lets slip by.

WHAT IS THE WORST SIN?

Let me ask you a question: which was David's greatest sin?

Was it his adultery with Bathsheba and the subsequent, treacherous murder of her loyal husband, Uriah? Or was it his conceited desire to have more than a million fighting men under his command?

Most Christians would say the first, without a moment's hesitation. After all, the only direct damage caused by the census was the blistering on Joab's feet. Counting does not hurt people. The sin began and ended inside David's own head. He was simply being vain.

By contrast, his stolen night with Bathsheba produced snowballing complications. His mistress became pregnant. Events then descended into farce as David, in a desperate attempt to conceal the pregnancy, brought Uriah home from the battlefront and tried unsuccessfully to get him into Bathsheba's bed. Finally, when Uriah, the good soldier, insisted on sleeping outside, David unceremoniously had him killed.

On the face of it, then, the taking of Bathsheba seems a far uglier, messier sin. It is more concrete. We can understand the psychology of it. It is, in biblical terms, a *sin of the flesh.*

But that is not the way God saw it. To God, the more serious sin was the sin of pride—a *sin of the spirit.* Just look at the punishments that followed. As a consequence of David's affair with Bathsheba, four people died. As a consequence of his numbering the army, "the LORD sent a plague on Israel, and seventy thousand men of Israel fell dead" (1 Chron. 21:14 NIV).

The most dangerous sins are not sins of the flesh, but sins of the spirit—for two very good reasons.

SINS OF THE SPIRIT—SATAN'S SPECIALTY

Satan specializes in these sins of the spirit, and he never calls in sick or takes a day off. He is always on the job.

In a small town in Nebraska lived a lady named Mrs. Thompson, who was renowned countywide for her godliness. It was common knowledge that nobody was so bad that she couldn't find something nice to say about him or her.

One day two young men were talking, and one of them said, "This is too good to be true. There must be someone Mrs. Thompson doesn't like."

"Nah," said the other one. "She gets along with everyone."

"I bet I know somebody she'll speak evil of," said the first.

"You're on."

So they went and knocked on Mrs. Thompson's door.

"Good morning, Mrs. Thompson," said the first young man, winking at the other. "I wonder if you'd tell me—what do you think about the devil?"

She cocked her head to one side like a parrot, and replied, "Well, there's one thing I'll say for him—he's always on the job!"

Mrs. Thompson was absolutely right. Satan, Lucifer, the devil—he has many names in Scripture. He is always on the job, and his job is trying to lead Christians into sin.

A lot of the time he uses trials and temptations of the kind we looked at in the last chapter. He tries to ignite our appetites—greed, envy, lust, for example. Or he tries to beat us into submission through fear of pain. In other words, much of Satan's stock-in-trade has to do with sins of the flesh. To which the appropriate response for Christians is to pray, "Lead us not into temptation."

But sins of the flesh are small potatoes to the devil. What he is really interested in are the more dangerous, more elusive sins of the spirit. Because that is the kind of sin that got him thrown out of heaven. And that is the kind of sin that gives him the tightest grasp on the human heart.

Read what Isaiah had to say about Satan:

> How you have fallen from heaven,
>   O morning star, son of the dawn!
> You have been cast down to the earth,

> you who once laid low the nations!
> You said in your heart,
>> "I will ascend to heaven;
> I will raise my throne
>> above the stars of God;
> I will sit enthroned on the mount of assembly,
>> on the utmost heights of the sacred mountain.
> I will ascend above the tops of the clouds;
>> I will make myself like the Most High."
> But you are brought down to the grave,
>> to the depths of the pit. (Isaiah 14:12–15 NIV)

Five times Satan uses the words "I will." It is Satan's obsession to be like God. He *will* "sit enthroned." He *will* raise his throne "above the stars of God." Deep in the center of Satan's sin is a spiritual pride so complete that it utterly ignores the facts. Already "brought down to the depths of the pit," Satan nevertheless hopes to snatch the Almighty's scepter.

He failed to do that in open warfare. So now he hopes to do it on the battlefield of the human will. He seeks to duplicate his own spiritual pride in the heart of every Christian on the planet. That is his goal. And he is utterly dedicated to accomplishing it.

Not surprisingly, then, Jesus does not only tell us to pray, "Lead us not into temptation." He immediately follows up with "Deliver us from evil." The New International Version has the most accurate translation: "Deliver us from the evil one."

That's how crucial a matter spiritual pride is.

SINS OF THE SPIRIT ARE "RESPECTABLE" SINS

The second reason sins of the spirit are especially dangerous is that Christians often see them as "respectable." We wink at them. We give them tacit approval.

Examine your reaction to current events.

When a Christian leader begins to relish the role of celebrity, we find it regrettable but excuse it as the almost inevitable consequence of media pressure. Only when that leader commits adultery or embezzles funds do we feel pushed into outright and unequivocal condemnation. It takes a concrete, flesh-centered sin to arouse our indignation.

Or examine the way you read Scripture.

Which part of the prodigal's story in Luke 15 do we recall most vividly? His sin and repentance. It's a perfectly symmetrical tale. He goes blundering off to squander his estate on wine, women, and song. Then times get hard, and he turns around and makes his penitential journey in the opposite direction. His flesh-based sin is cleanly repented of and forgiven when the prodigal returns to the farm. Everything's fixed.

Or is it? Sometimes we hardly bother to read the final chapter. And perhaps we do not read it because the older brother's complaint hits too close to home. After all, the older son had a point. What reward had he received for his years of faithful labor? Why was such a fuss being made over his precocious kid brother, when all the kid brother had done was waste the family inheritance? Wasn't he, the faithful one who had stayed home, the more deserving?

Do you recognize what's behind the older brother's complaint? Of course you do. It's *spiritual pride*.

I think the church has a real problem in this area because sins of pride are so insidious. It takes real effort to commit a sin of the flesh. You have to expend energy in the process of satisfying your cravings. The glutton has to empty the fridge. The adulterer has to set up his illicit rendezvous.

In contrast, sins of the spirit belong mainly in the mind. It's possible to be racked with spiritual pride, yet for that condition to be invisible to everyone else. Like cancer, the inner malaise will sooner or later manifest itself. But its roots are internal. You can have it—and still hide it.

As a result, we wholeheartedly, and rightly, condemn the fleshly sins. But we are less vocal about those spiritual sins we all quietly cling to. We go easy on the sins of the spirit. We go easy on pride. We go easy on stubbornness. We go easy on gossip. We go easy on envy and jealousy.

May God help us to wake up! As Paul advises, "Let us purify ourselves from everything that contaminates *body and spirit*, perfecting holiness out of reverence for God" (2 Cor. 7:1 NIV, emphasis mine).

GET A REALITY CHECK

Fundamentally, spiritual pride is a celebration of self. It is a trust in self. It is a preoccupation with self at the expense of others. And we all suffer from it.

- Every time you think yourself more intelligent than others—that is spiritual pride.

- Every time you think yourself to be the reason for your own business success—that is spiritual pride.

- Every time you think yourself more experienced in faith and more able at living the Christian life—that is spiritual pride.

- Every time you think yourself more humble than others—that is spiritual pride.

So how do we begin to let God answer the prayer, "Deliver us from the evil one"?

The answer is this: by doing a reality check.

Remember the time at the start of Jesus' ministry where the Spirit drove Him out into the wilderness to be tempted by Satan?

"Again, the devil took him to a very high mountain and showed him all the kingdoms of the world and their splendor. All this I will give you," he said, "if you will bow down and worship me" (Matt. 4:8–9 NIV).

Imagine yourself being offered a job like that: presidency over the entire known world. What a recognition of your talents! It's the kind of career break only a fool would turn down—a once-in-a-lifetime chance.

Or is it?

Jesus did not listen to the sales pitch. Instead He cut through to the essential issue. He ran a reality check on Satan's argument. He held it up against the measure of God's Word, and found it to be built on lies. "Jesus said to him, 'Away from me, Satan! For it is written, "Worship the Lord your God, and serve him only."' Then the devil left him, and angels came and attended him" (Matt. 4:10 NIV).

Believe me, if Satan did not spare the Lord Jesus Christ from this form of temptation, he is not going to spare you or me. I engage daily in hand-to-hand combat with Satan in exactly this area. Because the better things are going, the more prone we are to get slack and complacent.

It is no coincidence that David fell into spiritual pride at the very peak of his success. He was in good health. The kingdom was in great shape. He had learned his lesson about adultery. And so he rested on his laurels . . . and Satan slipped under his guard.

David should have been saying, "God has blessed me richly. I will continue to enjoy God's blessing as long as I trust in God and carry out my duties faithfully as king." That would have been a reality check.

If you want an example of how to do it *right*, just look at Jesus' mother, Mary. An angel visited her. God said He had chosen her to bear His only Son. What more fertile ground for spiritual pride could there be? What news to gossip around Galilee!

But Mary refused to budge from scriptural reality. "I am the Lord's servant," she said to the visiting angel. "May it be to me as you have said" (Luke 1:38 NIV). And later when she met her cousin Elizabeth, she showed not a hint of conceit: "My soul glorifies the Lord and my spirit rejoices in God my Savior, for he has been mindful of the humble state of his servant" (Luke 1:46–47 NIV).

This is what Peter had in mind when he gave early Christians this advice:

Clothe yourselves with humility toward one another, because,
"God opposes the proud
    but gives grace to the humble."
Humble yourselves, therefore, under God's mighty hand, that he may
lift you up in due time. (1 Peter 5:5–6 NIV)

Refuse to give yourself airs. That is the clear message of Scripture.

When God blesses you financially, don't fall into the trap of thinking you got rich by your own skill. Pray, "Deliver me from the evil one"—and then give the money away ruthlessly.

When God blesses you with a brilliant mind, don't fall into the trap of thinking you had something to do with it. Pray "Deliver me from the evil one"—and then use your clarity of thought without putting other people down.

When God blesses you with health and good looks, don't fall into the trap of scorning others as inferior. Pray, "Deliver me from the evil one"—and then use what God has given you in the service of the kingdom.

When God blesses you with opportunities to minister, don't fall into the trap of thinking you are the best thing to happen to the kingdom of God since the apostle Paul. Pray, "Deliver me from the evil one"—and focus on the goals God gives you.

When God blesses you with success in whatever you do, don't fall into the trap of thinking you deserve it. Pray, "Deliver me from the evil one"—and ask God for what purpose He has given you these endowments.

Finally, let me emphasize three things about deliverance from evil.

1. We are delivered from evil by the death and resurrection of the Lord Jesus Christ. By dying on Calvary, Jesus saved us not only from the penalty of sin—which is eternal torment—but also from the power of sin.

Jesus has given us every resource we need to overcome Satan. We will succeed if we refuse to take an exaggerated view of our own importance, and if we do not try to battle it out in temptation when we ought to have made a strategic retreat. Martin Luther warned: "When temptation knocks on the door, send Jesus to answer it."

Only believers in the Lord Jesus Christ can pray with confidence the words, "Deliver us from the evil one." In effect we are saying, "Lord, you have delivered me from the evil one eternally—now deliver me daily."

2. We are delivered from the evil one because of Jesus' intercession on our behalf. We are never alone in temptation, though that is the impression Satan would dearly love to give us. As Hebrews tells us, Jesus "is able to save completely those who come to God through him, because he always lives to intercede for them" (Heb. 7:25 NIV). Everywhere you go, whatever state you're in, you enjoy Jesus' constant intercession. When you pray, "Deliver me from the evil one," Jesus is already asking the Father for this to happen.

3. Praying "deliver us from evil" is much easier when you do it in fellowship with other believers. The community of believers belongs together. Faith is not just a covenant with God—it is a covenant with our brothers and sisters in Christ. When we receive baptism, we are received also into the fellowship of believers.

Church is more than a bunch of individuals who come together on Sundays ten minutes late. It is a community of those bought by the blood of Jesus Christ, and who feel a deep sense of responsibility to one another. In the church we are united for mutual encouragement, mutual accountability, and mutual prayer support.

Anyone who has lived in a family will know how effectively our loved ones can puncture pride—yet without threatening our security. The same thing should happen in God's family. "Deliver *us* from the evil one," we are told to pray. In no other line of the Lord's Prayer is that plural so important.

PRAYER
WORKBOOK

TO REFLECT ON:

As a starting point, think about two areas in which spiritual pride could be a problem for you. Identify what exactly that pride in yourself focuses on—a particular quality, a particular role, or a particular accomplishment. Be as frank as you can. I have written down two areas where I often confront spiritual pride. Put your answers in the spaces that follow.

MY ANSWERS

1. Preaching what will make people feel good instead of wanting to be good.
2. Anger toward liberals and apostates, and wanting to see them vanish.

YOUR ANSWERS

1. _____

_____

2. _____

_____

We can begin to tackle spiritual pride by doing a reality check against Scripture. For each of the areas you identified above, write a statement, drawn from the truth of God's Word, that puts your roles and qualities and accomplishments in proper perspective. Are you really the master of your own ship—or do you need to remind yourself of your complete dependence on God?

MY ANSWERS

1. Continually coming under the lordship of Christ and acknowledging the need to be like Him.
2. Remembering often that God is in control—and that my job is to preach His truth.

YOUR ANSWERS

1. _____

_____

2. _____

_____

TO READ:

Spend a few minutes quietly reflecting on these Scriptures:

> For by the grace given me I say to every one of you: Do not think of yourself more highly than you ought, but rather think of yourself with sober judgment, in accordance with the measure of faith God has given you. Just as each of us has one body with many members, and these members do not all have the same function, so in Christ we who are many form one body, and each member belongs to all the others. (Rom. 12:3–5 NIV)

> When God saw what they did and how they turned from their evil ways, he had compassion and did not bring upon them the destruction he had threatened.

But Jonah was greatly displeased and became angry. He prayed to the LORD, "O LORD, is this not what I said when I was still at home? That is why I was so quick to flee to Tarshish. I knew that you are a gracious and compassionate God, slow to anger and abounding in love, a God who relents from sending calamity. Now O LORD, take away my life, for it is better for me to die than to live." (Jonah 3:10, 4:1–3 NIV)

> He has showed you, O man, what is good.
> And what does the LORD require of you?
> To act justly and to love mercy
> and to walk humbly with your God. (Mic. 6:8 NIV)

TO PRAY:

Finally, take a legal pad. Collect all your thoughts and write a prayer that enables you to confront and deal with spiritual pride. As before, avoid using "stock phrases." Make sure that everything you thank God for, and everything you ask Him for, comes from your heart and has meaning for you personally. Make the prayer as long or as short as you wish. When you are satisfied with it, copy it into this book. Then spend a little time quietly in the presence of your heavenly Father before speaking it out loud. This is my prayer. Write yours in the space that follows.

MY PRAYER

Father, the evil one never rests, and he always prowls around like a roaring lion. His sin of rebellion threw him out of heaven. His tempting of Adam and Eve with the same sin threw them out of the Garden. While I know that You will never throw me out of Your presence, I know that falling into his temptation will separate me from the joy and the peace that comes from sweet fellowship with You.

You have given me the full armor of God to stand against the evil one. Help me today to put on all my armor, so that his fiery darts may fizzle out.

I don't want to wander away from closeness to You, and yet that is the evil one's intention for me today. He will try to accomplish this ever so subtly and slowly. He will try to get me away from Christian fellowship with other believers, away from worshiping You. Deliver me from this master manipulator, and give me discernment today—spiritual discernment to see what You see and think what You think.

Deliver me today from human wisdom that comes from the evil one.

Deliver me today from worldly pressures that may come from well-meaning Christians.

Deliver me today from my own propensity for self-deception.

YOUR PRAYER

_____

_____

_____

_____

_____

_____

_____

_____

_____

_____

_____

_____

_____

_____

"The Kingdom and the Power"

11

Power to the People

On a recent tour of Scotland I walked through the historic town of St. Andrews. Its largest church building lies in the center—a huge stone edifice within easy reach of every resident. Inside I discovered seating for well over a thousand.

I imagined the place full on a Sunday morning. It must have been quite a sight—all those people gathered for the glory of God in such a splendid architectural setting.

Turning to my host—a friend connected to St. Andrews University, who had lived in the town for many years—I asked if he had worshiped here.

"Are you kidding?" he said. "You know how many people attend this church on Sunday morning?"

I confessed I did not know.

"Six."

I thought I had misheard him. "*Six?*"

"To be exact, six elderly ladies. The only time they even half fill this place is when a local school wants to hold a special assembly."

I looked around the building with fresh eyes. Magnificent it certainly was. But the splendor of it counted for nothing—it was a mere shell. Like an ancient Chevrolet up on blocks, it sat there looking beautiful in its faded glory, but completely unable to move.

It was a church bereft of power.

THE POWER OF THE EARLY CHURCH

Power is a popular word in America.

It reminds us of huge, well-oiled machinery turning iron ore into steel girders. We talk about media power, political power, economic power. We don't just have lunches—we have power lunches. We don't just have breakfasts—we have power breakfasts. We don't just talk—we have power talks. Power intoxicates us. We can't get enough of it.

And there's a lot of *rhetoric* about power in the church. The power of God, the power of the gospel, the power of prayer. But here is an odd thing: beneath all the big phrases, it is remarkably difficult to find any real power.

Where is the power that—almost literally—ought to spark from Christians when they get together?

Well, nowhere that I can see.

Yet church ought to be about life-transforming power.

Read what Jesus said to His disciples the last time He met them on earth:

> He told them, "This is what is written: The Christ will suffer and rise from the dead on the third day, and repentance and forgiveness of sins will be preached in his name to all nations, beginning at Jerusalem. You are witnesses of these things. I am going to send you what my Father has promised; but stay in the city until you have been clothed with power from on high." (Luke 24:46–49 NIV)

Clothed with power from on high. The power the New Testament church enjoyed came directly from God. Being locked in that upper room in Jerusalem did not give it to them. Being in fellowship together did not give it to them. Even knowing that Jesus had been raised from the dead did not give it to them.

The power belonged to the Holy Spirit.

Some of its effects were dramatic. The ability to speak in different languages. The power to cure illness. But these miracles were the froth spilling over the side of the glass. The bulk of the power energized the disciples from within; it gave supernatural edge to their mission of preaching Christ to the nations.

What, we often wonder, could have moved three thousand people to join the church on the day the Holy Spirit was outpoured? The answer is *power*. It was not just the message of the resurrection that impacted the world—indeed the message itself was often met with derision by the crowds. But the empowerment of the disciples never failed to leave its mark.

"When they saw the courage of Peter and John and realized that they were unschooled, ordinary men, they were astonished, and they took note that these men had been with Jesus" (Acts 4:13 NIV).

In the New Testament church, riot and revival seemed to go hand in hand. Believers were stoned to death. Later they were thrown to the lions. Yet the power of God continued to grip them, and consequently the gospel burned like a brush fire across the entire Roman world.

People in the early church did not get bored. But things are different now. Sometimes it seems that we look for things to do so we can fill the hole left behind by the absence of the divine power. Why doesn't the same power run through us as ran through the early believers?

- They did not care much about church programs—though modern Baptists do.

- They did not care much about social action—though modern Methodists feel strongly about it.

- They did not care much about order and dignity—though modern Presbyterians are big on that.

- They did not care much about shouting—though modern Pentecostals often make it a priority.

- They did not care much about ritual—though modern Catholics, Episcopalians, and Lutherans can't do without it.

I apologize if I offend you. But this is very, very important. I read in Scripture that it is God's will for the church of the Lord Jesus Christ to have power. Supernatural and delivering power. Power to pull down the strongholds of Satan in people's lives. Power to break the chains of misery and habit. Power to convert and conquer and convict of sin. Power to uplift people and give them a foretaste of heaven.

"The kingdom of God," Paul says emphatically, "is not a matter of talk but of power" (1 Cor. 4:20 NIV). God wants his church to have that power—and use it.

So what went wrong? Why did the Church lose its power?

WHO TURNED THE POWER OFF?

At the turn of the nineteenth century, a lady lived alone in a house on Scotland's west coast. Being a traditional Scot, she tended to be frugal. It surprised her neighbors, therefore, when she announced one day, "I am going to have electricity put in my home."

They were shocked. At that time having electricity in your house was about as common as owning your own nuclear reactor is today—and in most things this lady could hardly be called an innovator! But she kept her word, and a few weeks later the power lines were linked up. She was one of the first Electricity Board customers in town.

But then something strange happened.

When the meter reading came due, the Electricity Board sent one of its employees to her door. He read her meter and noted the numbers down. And then he frowned.

"Is your electricity working?" he asked.

"Yes," she replied. "It's working wonderfully. Is something wrong?"

He shook his head. "It's just that your meter shows you've scarcely used any electricity at all—and you've had it now for three months."

But at that the lady laughed.

"Oh, that's easily explained," she said. "You see, I don't need very much of it. Every evening when the sun sets, I turn the electric lamps on just long enough to light my candle. And then I turn them off again!"

Many of today's Christians are exactly like that frugal lady.

We are wired up for power—but we're not using it. Our souls are saved—but our hearts are unchanged. We are spiritually connected—but it has not registered in our lifestyle. We have trusted the Lord Jesus Christ for salvation—but we resist transformation.

True, we occasionally flip on the switch. But we only leave it on long enough to light our own little candles. And as a result, we spend most of our Christian life in the shadows. Most of the amazing potential of divine power we never utilize.

But why sing, "There is power, power, wonder-working power in the blood of the Lamb"—when, thirty minutes after the service ends, we have forgotten all about God's power, and we are once again using our own wimpy little batteries?

The fact is, today's Christians rarely rely on the power of the Holy Spirit. We have become insipid and weak because we refuse to let God's power in. We put our own priorities first. We make the effort to serve God—*if* it's convenient. We make the effort to change—*if* it fits our lifestyle. Dig down inside yourself, and it won't be too long before you find a hard core of self-interest.

And that just won't wash with God.

DON'T DELAY THE CHURCH

In the late 1970s we lived in Pasadena, California—just one block away from Colorado Boulevard, where the Tournament of Roses Parade took place every New Year's Day.

During one of those events, one of the most beautiful floats suddenly sputtered and quit. You can imagine what happened. The entire parade ground to a halt behind it. Everything had to wait half an hour while somebody went to find a can of gas big enough to fill the tank.

But here's the irony: that fancy float belonged to the Standard Oil Company. For all its vast reserves of oil around the globe, Standard Oil could not keep its own float moving down the street. It looked great, but it had turned into a roadblock.

Great-looking roadblocks are common in congregations today. Because Christians who refuse to live in and by God's power end up delaying the whole church. You can't drag your feet and expect other people to carry you along.

Those who are not delighting themselves in the Lord are delaying the church. They may be saved, but they're stalling. The mess America is in as a nation owes a lot to the fact that God's people have ceased to trust in the power of God. And we are making it worse by resorting to the world's techniques instead of letting the world stand in awe of what God can do through His people.

The Lord is looking for those who will be united in bringing glory to His name.

How can we do it?

How to Get the Power Flowing

Look again at the example of the New Testament church.

On their visit to Philippi, Paul and Silas got into deep trouble:

The crowd joined in the attack against Paul and Silas, then the magistrates ordered them to be stripped and beaten. After they had been severely flogged, they were thrown into prison, and the jailer was commanded to guard them carefully. Upon receiving such orders, he put them in the inner cell and fastened their feet in the stocks.

About midnight Paul and Silas were praying and singing hymns to

God, and the other prisoners were listening to them. Suddenly there was such a violent earthquake that the foundations of the prison were shaken. At once all the prison doors flew open, and everybody's chains came loose. The jailer woke up, and when he saw the prison doors open, he drew his sword and was about to kill himself because he thought the prisoners had escaped. But Paul shouted, "Don't harm yourself! We are all here!"

The jailer called for lights, rushed in and fell trembling before Paul and Silas. He then brought them out and asked, "Sirs, what must I do to be saved?" (Acts 16:22–30 NIV)

This was not a situation most of us would relish. Unjustly arrested, Paul and Silas had been dragged before the magistrates on a trumped-up charge, then flogged and shackled in a central room of the prison.

We should not allow the intervening centuries to romanticize our view of what happened. This was police brutality. The flogging hurt every bit as much as being worked over with baseball bats by a couple of thugs in the KGB. There was nothing picturesque about it. This was not a pillow fight. They could have died.

After such treatment, most Christians would feel pretty sorry for themselves. They would be wishing they had never included this town in their itinerary. Wishing they had kept their mouths closed instead of preaching. They would lay short odds on never seeing the light of day again.

Under far less provocation than this, believers like you and me have folded. We would have given up on the power of God and settled for trying to save our skins.

But not Paul and Silas.

Come midnight, according to Luke, they were "praying and singing hymns to God." It was as though the prison and its chains did not exist. Ignoring the pain and the danger, they set about the business of witnessing to the other prisoners. As far as we know, they did not even pray, "Lead us not into temptation" or "Please get us out of here, Lord."

All they did was *praise God.*

The praise released the power—and the power released Paul and Silas.

To be precise, the outpouring of God's power manifested in the earthquake put control of the situation back into their hands. First they prevented the jailer from taking his own life. And later, when the magistrates found out they were Roman citizens and wanted to release them quietly, Paul and Silas insisted that the magistrates personally escort them out of prison.

Praise and power go together, because the attitude of praise opens us up to God. Indeed, the close presence of God cannot help but draw praise from us. When Jesus rode into Jerusalem and the crowds came out to meet Him with their palm branches, some of the Pharisees complained, "Teacher rebuke your disciples." Jesus' response was: "I tell you, if they keep quiet, the stones will cry out" (Luke 19:39–40 NIV).

The Lord's Prayer—the prayer that God will answer—is a prayer supported by praise. Jesus taught us to begin our prayers by saying, "Hallowed be Your name," and to end them by affirming "Yours is the kingdom and the power and the glory forever."

That focus on praising God underlies everything else. We need to go on "emptying ourselves of ourselves" so that we can receive God's power. We need to get rid of self-seeking, get rid of self-sensitivity, get rid of self-pity. We need, in fact, to subdue everything associated with self.

Then, and only then, will we begin to experience God's power working through us.

THE COMING KINGDOM

Let me return for a moment to that Scottish church I mentioned at the beginning of this chapter. Astonished at its decline, I asked my friend in St. Andrews how a church that must once have housed a thriving congregation could shrivel down to a meager assembly of six old ladies.

His reply was revealing.

"Twenty years ago," he said, "the minister and the organist had an argument. And they never patched it up. Since that day they have never spoken a word to one another."

It boggled my mind how the minister and his director of music could function without talking. "Do they communicate at all?" I asked.

"Oh yes," my friend said. "Every Sunday the minister comes into church early, and he leaves a note with that day's hymns on the organ. The organist comes in just before the service starts. He plays all the hymns with his back to the minister. And as soon as he hears the last amen, he leaves."

I still cannot quite believe that two church leaders could preside over such catastrophic decline. Satan must be laughing.

But it illustrates a crucial point.

Praise has a strong *corporate* dimension. Paul and Silas singing hymns *together* released the power of God. And in St. Andrews, the animosity between the two men in charge of the church effectively prevented any expression of praise at all. Whatever hymns the organist played and the six elderly ladies sang, they didn't amount to praise.

In church after church across Europe and America, I have seen the same telltale signs of decline. People who insist on being too "dignified" to praise God, and who tell you their faith is a "private matter." So private, apparently, that not even God is allowed in on it.

Yet in heaven, where praise is perfect and constant, there will be no place for disagreement or disharmony of spirit. Jesus will not establish a democracy but a kingdom. Democracy is the best we can do in a world split into ethnic, social, and economic factions. But in heaven we will go beyond democracy to the perfect rule of God.

Jesus will not ask for your vote. He will not take Gallup polls to find out what people want. He will not assemble a panel of experts and scholars to advise Him. He will not negotiate with this or that group in order to "keep them on board." There will be no dialogue through the World Council of Churches.

When Jesus comes, He will reign in power and glory and unassailable wisdom—and it will be *great*.

THE PRAYER THAT GOD WILL ANSWER

Until then, the Church should go on praising God and praying in the manner He taught us.

However, I sometimes imagine the Lord Jesus looking down on this world He died for. And I think how much it must grieve Him to see all the sin and deception, the wickedness and dishonesty, the willful confusion of evil and good. For despite our sophistication, this world is little better than the one Noah saw vanish under the waters of the flood.

Then I think of Jesus looking down on his bride, the Church. What does He see? Sadly—in most cases—halfhearted commitment, lack of love, preoccupation with the things of earth, stubbornness and self-serving, arrogance and pride. Can this truly be the bride He will return to earth to marry?

Then I imagine Him looking down and seeing His faithful people. People who praise Him with all their hearts, thank Him and adore Him with all their strength, honor Him with all their resources. These are the ones who bring joy to God's heart. These are the ones who focus on Him.

And these are the ones who, because they focus on Him daily, can pray the prayer that He will answer.

I trust you are not in the first group. I hope you're not in the second. And I pray that the third group may receive the blessing that is their due.

PRAYER
WORKBOOK

TO REFLECT ON:

As a starting point, think about the times you have seen God's power made real in your life, or in the life of your church. Then think of two areas where you would like God's power to be more evident. What do you most want God to accomplish in you and your Christian brothers and sisters? I have written down two areas in which I'd like to see God's power displayed in The Church of the Apostles. Put your answers in the spaces that follow.

MY ANSWERS

1. That thousands of additional men and women may come and discover the saving knowledge of the Lord Jesus Christ.
2. That these individuals will be equipped by the power of God's Word and Spirit to go out and reach more of the lost.

YOUR ANSWERS

1. _____

2. _____

Praise releases power. Think of some occasions in the past when you have praised God, and then identify two ways in which you can bring praise alive in your walk with God. What makes you want to praise Him? In what ways can you express your praise? How can you keep praise vital even at times you feel distressed and challenged?

MY ANSWERS

1. I use praise music to first get my heart warmed up and help focus my thoughts on God.
2. I learn how to expand the kingdom through the power of praise.

YOUR ANSWERS

1. _____

   _____

2. _____

   _____

TO READ:
Spend a few minutes quietly reflecting on these Scriptures:

> Who is like the LORD our God,
>   the One who sits enthroned on high,
> who stoops down to look
>   on the heavens and the earth?
> He raises the poor from the dust
>   and lifts the needy from the ash heap;
> he seats them with princes,
>   with the princes of their people.
> He settles the barren woman in her home
>   as a happy mother of children.
>   Praise the LORD. (Ps. 113:5–9 NIV)

To keep me from becoming conceited because of these surpassingly great revelations, there was given me a thorn in my flesh, a messenger of Satan, to torment me. Three times I pleaded with the Lord to take it away from me. But he said to me, "My grace is sufficient for you, for my power is made perfect in weakness." Therefore I will boast all the more gladly about my weaknesses, so that Christ's power may rest on me. That is why, for Christ's sake, I delight in weaknesses, in insults, in hardships, in persecutions, in difficulties. For when I am weak, then I am strong. (2 Cor. 12:7–10 NIV)

Then a voice came from the throne, saying:
"Praise our God,
    all you servants,
you who fear him,
    both small and great!"

Then I heard what sounded like a great multitude, like the roar of rushing waters and like loud peals of thunder, shouting:
"Hallelujah!
    For our Lord God Almighty reigns.
Let us rejoice and be glad
    and give him glory!
For the wedding of the Lamb has come,
    and his bride has made herself ready.
Fine linen, bright and clean,
    was given her to wear." (Rev. 19:5–8 NIV)

TO PRAY:

Finally, take a legal pad. Collect all your thoughts and write a prayer that helps you leave self aside and focus on the glory and power of God. As before, avoid using "stock phrases." Make sure that everything you thank God for, and everything you ask Him for, comes from your heart and has meaning for you personally. Make the prayer as long or as short as you wish. When you are satisfied with it, copy it into this book. Then spend a little time quietly in the presence of your heavenly Father before speaking it out loud. This is my prayer. Write yours in the space that follows.

MY PRAYER

Father, today I want to be reminded constantly that all the power and the glory are Yours.

That I can do nothing without Your power.

That I am ineffective without Your power.

That I cannot accomplish Your will without Your power.

Today, Father, I want to bring glory to Your name.

Let Your name be glorified—in my words, in my actions, in my decisions, in my thought processes.

Today let those who will see the work of my hands or hear the words of my lips say what an awesome God I worship—not what a good person I am.

For to You alone is the power, glory, majesty, dominion, and authority, forever and ever. Amen.

YOUR PRAYER

_____

_____

_____

_____

_____

_____

_____

12

Praying the Prayer
That God Answers:
Your Daily Guide

Now that you have finished this in-depth study of the Lord's Prayer—
the prayer that God will answer—how do you incorporate what you
have learned into your regular prayer time? To help you, I have included
a daily prayer guide for your use.

The ten-step guide is a brief summary of this book. Ideally, you
will pray through all ten steps each day. Realistically, that may not
be possible. Continue to work through the steps until you have
absorbed the pattern, and you will soon find yourself praying in this
manner spontaneously.

Leading The Way offers this daily prayer guide in a handy booklet
that you can put in your Bible to use during your devotions. To order
a copy of this practical prayer guide, call our toll-free number, 1-800-
337-5323, or visit our Web site at www.leadingtheway.org. Ask for the
booklet *A Daily Guide to Experiencing Power in Prayer* (BL#0019).

Step One:
Recognizing Your Father

"Our Father"

Our heavenly Father is not a cold, distant, angry father. He is our Daddy, one with whom we can have an intimate, joyful relationship. He is attentive to our needs 100 percent of the time. He becomes our Daddy only through repentance and faith in Jesus Christ.

In prayer acknowledge that . . .

- God is your heavenly Daddy and He loves you more than you can ever imagine.

- He accepts you, forgives you, and restores you.

- He removes your fears, gives you hope, and becomes your dearest companion.

- You are often like the rebellious prodigal son or his self-righteous brother.

In Prayer Today: Thank your heavenly Daddy for your priceless, intimate relationship with Him. Come to Him as a little child comes to his father. Thank Him today for one of the qualities He demonstrates as a Father: His love, grace, mercy, patience, and quickness to forgive. Sing a praise chorus or listen to worship music.

Step Two:
Longing to Be with Him

"In Heaven"

God lives in heaven, but He also lives in your heart. You can experience heaven here and now.

Remember that heaven is . . .

- your Daddy's native environment

- filled with the presence of your Savior

- a place where you will experience no death, no separation, no sorrow, no crying, no painful memories

- where you will be free from Satan's temptations and sin

In Prayer Today: Take a moment to contemplate what heaven is. Thank God for what He has in store for you there. Ask God to prepare you to live with Him in heaven. Ask Him to help you experience heaven in your life today.

Step Three:
Honoring His Name

"HALLOWED BE YOUR NAME"

In Bible times, a person's name explained who that person was. A name was one of a person's most prized possessions. This was doubly true of God. His name was foremost in people's prayers.

Prayer turns our eyes away from ourselves to honor God's person, identity, character, and reputation. Through our prayers, we build a house for God to dwell in.

Prayer honors God for being . . .

- pure

- compassionate

- righteous and just

- merciful

- honest

- faithful

In Prayer Today: Thank God for every facet of His character. Each day, focus on a different facet. Ask God to help you honor Him today with your lips, giving of your substance, and your obedience to Him.

Step Four:
Pledging Allegiance to
His Kingdom

"Your Kingdom Come"

When you accept Christ as your Savior, you are adopted into the kingdom of God. Citizenship in His kingdom confers tremendous rights and privileges but also demands responsibilities.

God invites you into His kingdom. In turn, you . . .

- invite His kingdom to dominate every facet of your life—your plans, your friends, your marriage, your children, your job, your career

- surrender yourself to God and ask Him to dethrone Satan

- pray that God's kingdom will come to the lost, setting them free from Satan's bondage

- eagerly wait for Jesus' second coming

In Prayer Today: Reaffirm your allegiance to God's kingdom and submit every area of your life to His control. Name one area that you especially need to submit to God today, and ask Him to help you surrender it. Pray for one lost person who needs to be freed from Satan's grasp. Thank God that Jesus is coming again!

Step Five:
Seeking His Will

"YOUR WILL BE DONE"

In His Word, God reveals much of what He wants us to do, but we must continue to trust Him daily for guidance in those gray areas. Our focus should be on God's will, God's name, and God's kingdom, not on our own needs.

Doing God's will means that you . . .

- consciously ask that His will be done in every area of your life

- seek His glory and His honor

- trust Him to do what is best for you

In Prayer Today: Ask God to help you focus on what He wants you to do today. Focus on one area of your life—your family, your job, your relationships—where you need to seek His will. Tell Him you want Him to be glorified in every action, word, and thought today. Thank Him for looking out for your best interests.

Step Six:
Trusting Him to Meet
Your Needs

"Our Daily Bread"

God tells us to make Him our number one priority, and He has promised to make us His top priority. We are not to be consumed or obsessed with physical needs. When we worry about our needs, we are saying that we do not believe God will really provide for us.

Trusting God means . . .

- to refrain from worry and anxiety

- to recognize that His priority is to take care of you

- to trust completely in His promise to meet your needs

- to petition Him to meet those needs

In Prayer Today: Tell God you want to make Him your top priority. Thank Him for His promise to take care of your every need. Thank Him for His provision. Think of one specific area of need today and thank God that He will handle it for you.

Step Seven:
Forgiving Others

"Forgive Us . . . As We Also Have Forgiven"

God's Word tells us that when we accept Christ, we become His children permanently. But as we walk through life, we become soiled daily with sin. One way to experience forgiveness ourselves is through forgiving others. God is delighted when we forgive others.

Being a Christian means that you . . .

- daily recognize your need for cleansing

- must confess your sins to your Daddy, and thank Him for His cleansing

- forgive others to the same extent that you have been forgiven

In Prayer Today: Thank God for His endless forgiveness. Ask Him to demonstrate His divine nature in you today by helping you forgive others. Think of one person who has wronged you in the past day or two. Pray right now that God will help you forgive him or her. Pray that God will bless that person.

Step Eight:
Developing Character
Through Testing

"Lead Us Not into Temptation"

Confusion comes when we fail to distinguish between temptation and testing. Temptation comes from Satan or our fleshly nature and leads to sin and disobedience. Testing comes from God to develop our character and results in glory to Him.

Temptation . . .

- enters our lives through those areas that are not surrendered to God's control

- starts with confusing our will with God's will, then appeals to our natural desires, and finally persuades us to disobey God

- brings shame and discouragement and the feeling that there is no use in trying to repent

In Prayer Today: As you pray today, yield totally to God's control so the enemy has no foothold in your life. Think of one area where Satan usually tempts you. Ask God to help you recognize and resist Satan's tactics in that area. Ask God to transform that temptation into a test, and to build your godly character when facing difficulty.

Step Nine:
Delivering Your Heart
from Pride

"Deliver Us from the Evil One"

Sin entered the world when Satan tried to exalt himself above God. When Satan tempted Adam and Eve, he tempted them to disobey God. He appealed to their wills and persuaded them to join him in his pride against Almighty God. Pride is a sin of the spirit.

God's Word tells us . . .

- pride is behind every sin we commit

- total surrender to God moment by moment is the only antidote to pride

- Jesus intercedes daily for us as we face temptation

In Prayer Today: Take a moment to confess your pride to the Lord. Think of one area in which you are likely to be puffed up with pride today. Pray that God will help you resist Satan's attempts to make you proud. Tell your heavenly Daddy once more that you surrender yourself to His control. Thank Jesus that He is interceding for you today.

Step Ten:
Praising God for His Power

"The Kingdom and the Power"

If we do not rely on the power of the Holy Spirit, we become weak and ineffective. Praise will get the power flowing in our lives. Praise and power go together, because the attitude of praise opens us up to God. Jesus taught us to begin our prayers with praise—"Hallowed be Your name"—and to end them with praise—"for Yours is the kingdom and the power and the glory."

God wants us to experience His power . . .

- for salvation through faith in Christ

- over sickness and disease

- over habits that enslave us

- to combat Satan's temptations and activities

In Prayer Today: Thank God for His vast power. Give Him glory for placing His resources at your disposal. Confess to Him that you often depend on your own power instead of His. Identify one area in your life today where you need His power, and ask Him to exhibit His power in that area.

About the Author

DR. MICHAEL YOUSSEF is the founding pastor of The Church of The Apostles in Atlanta, Georgia. This interdenominational evangelical church was founded in May 1987. It began with fewer than forty adults and has grown to nearly two thousand members today.

Dr. Youssef completed an undergraduate degree in theology at Moore Theological College in Sydney, Australia. He served for several years in pastoral ministry in Australia before emigrating to the United States, where he earned a master's degree in theology at Fuller Theological Seminary in 1978. He later earned his doctorate in social anthropology at Emory University.

In 1977, Dr. Youssef became a consultant to The Haggai Institute for Advanced Leadership Training. He rose to the position of managing director of The Haggai Institute and traveled worldwide training Christian leaders in evangelism and discipleship until 1987.

Dr. Youssef is the author of eleven books, the best known of which is *The Leadership Style of Jesus*, which has been translated into seven languages.

Dr. Youssef is married to the former Elizabeth Bailey, and they have four grown children and 7 grandchildren.

Leading The Way is Dr. Youssef's radio ministry. The mission of Leading The Way is to take the gospel of Jesus Christ to the lost. Dr. Youssef teaches the whole counsel of the Word of God and seeks to help people understand the authority of Scripture in every area of life.

The daily English-language program is aired in hundreds of communities throughout North America and in Belize, Central America. It is also beamed by satellite into the United Kingdom.

An English-Arabic program is broadcast several times each week over Trans World Radio facilities targeted to the Middle East and North Africa. The international ministry is expanding to other major languages of the world as well.

For information about the release of Leading The Way in your community, call our toll-free number, 1-800-337-5323, and request a copy of our station list. Or, visit our Web site at www.leadingtheway.org for a complete listing of all stations that carry Leading The Way. When you visit the Web site, you may want to listen to current or past programs on-line. You can also find us at OnePlace.com. For further information, write us at Leading The Way with Dr. Michael Youssef, P.O. Box 20100, Atlanta, Georgia 30325.